Honorable Mention, American Horticultural Society Book Awards

"Helping gardeners across the prairies succeed in growing food, flowers and everything in between" —*Medicine Hat News*

"Melrose and Normandeau answer all the questions that the two experts could think of when it came to horticulture on the prairies." —*Edify Edmonton*

"The Prairie Gardener's series offers knowledgeable yet accessible answers to questions covering a broad range of topics to help you cultivate garden success. Get growing!" —Lorene Edwards Forkner, gardener and author of *Color In and Out of the Garden*

"This is a beautiful and incredibly well-written series of books on earth-friendly gardening. Lavishly illustrated, with photos in every segment, the books are a pleasure just to leaf through, but the accessible writing and level of expertise makes them essential to any gardener's library. Although they're geared to prairie gardeners, I found great information that transfers anywhere, including where I live, in the Sierra Foothills, and will enjoy them for years to come. Well-indexed, to help you find solutions to elusive problems. Highly recommended!" —Diane Miessler, certified permaculture designer and author of *Grow Your Soil!*

"All your gardening questions answered! Reading the Prairie Gardener's series is like sitting down with your friendly local master gardener. Delivers practical guidance that will leave you feeling confident and inspired." —Andrea Bellamy, author of *Small-Space Vegetable Gardens*

"The Prairie Gardener's Go-To series comes in mighty yet digestible volumes covering popular topics like seeds, vegetables, and soil. These question-and-answer styled books get to the root of the matter with Janet and Sheryl's unique wit and humor. Although each guide touches on regionally specific information, the wisdom of these seasoned gardeners applies to any garden, wherever it may be." —Acadia Tucker, author of *Growing Perennial Foods*

T0017199

JANET MELROSE &
SHERYL NORMANDEAU

The Prairie Gardener's
Go-To for
Grasses

TOUCHWOOD

TouchWood Editions
touchwoodeditions.com

The information in this book is true and complete to the best of the authors' knowledge. All recommendations are made without guarantee on the part of the authors or the publisher.

Copy edited by Paula Marchese

Proofread by Meg Yamamoto

Designed by Tree Abraham

Photos by Janet Melrose and Sheryl Normandeau with the following exceptions:
p. 20 (Nancy J. Ondra / shutterstock.com), p. 25 (MD_style / shutterstock.com), p. 36 (ahmydaria / shutterstock.com), p. 43 (Zoom Team / shutterstock.com), p. 76 (Edda Dupree / istockphoto.com), p. 81 (Uellue / shutterstock.com), p. 85 (courtesy of Rob Normandy), p. 98 (fotoblend / pixabay.com), p. 122 (Dorofieiev / shutterstock.com), p. 125 (Gonzalo de Miceu / shutterstock.com), p. 130 (courtesy of Marina Matthes).

CATALOGUING DATA AVAILABLE FROM LIBRARY AND ARCHIVES CANADA

ISBN 9781771514309 (print)

ISBN 9781771514316 (electronic)

TouchWood Editions acknowledges that the land on which we live and work is within the traditional territories of the Lkwungen (Esquimalt and Songhees), Malahat, Pacheedaht, Scia'new, T'sou-ke, and WSÁNEĆ (Pauquachin, Tsartlip, Tsawout, and Tseycum) peoples.

We acknowledge the financial support of the Government of Canada through the Canada Book Fund, and the province of British Columbia through the Book Publishing Tax Credit.

This book was produced using FSC®-certified, acid-free papers, processed chlorine free, and printed with soya-based inks.

Printed in China

28 27 26 25 24 1 2 3 4 5

Dedicated to all prairie gardeners

Introduction

Grasses are a varied group. There are tall ones, short ones, ones that grow in water, and those that prefer dry land. Those that we walk on and those that we eat. A few are bulbs but most are not. Some have what we instantly recognize as flowers, but most do not. In short, they are as diverse a group as you could hope for.

Grasses serve many purposes in natural ecosystems and in our gardens. They provide habitat and food for wildlife and insects, and, in some cases, places to reproduce and raise young. Grasses can help with erosion control by providing a living cover. They beautify our spaces. Many grass species can tolerate drought in landscapes where water use is restricted. In *The Prairie Gardener's Go-To for Grasses*, we explore the fascinating and complex world of grasses, from the turf (or turf alternatives) that makes up your lawn to annual and perennial ornamental grasses that make statements in your garden as focal points, in borders, or planted in containers to showstopping effect. We even give you some ideas about grasses that you can eat!

Pull up a chair and explore the world of grasses with us!

Confidently designing a landscape that incorporates grasses takes a little inspiration and know-how, and we're here to guide you through the whole process. And when it comes to caring for and maintaining your garden grasses, we offer useful tips that will lead you to success. Most importantly, we encourage you to have fun growing this exciting group of plants and experimenting with different varieties in your garden. Let's get started! —SHERYL NORMANDEAU & JANET MELROSE

What are grasses?

Botanically speaking, as well as strictly speaking, grasses are relatively low, green, non-woody plants that belong to the 10,000-species-strong grass family (Poaceae).[1] Many definitions of what grasses are also include members of the rush (Juncaceae) and sedge (Cyperaceae) families as they are closer botanically to Poaceae than other plant families.

The reason is that members of these families are all monocots, with distinct morphological differences from dicots, those plant families we usually favour for our gardens. A monocot seed contains an embryo with one cotyledon (seed leaf) instead of the two that dicot species have. Hence the names monocotyledon[2] and dicotyledon, or monocot and dicot for short. Monocots also have roots that are adventitious, developing from nodes, whereas dicot roots develop from a radicle root and branch out from there. Monocots are all fibrous rooted, but dicots have a taproot. Monocots have stamens and petals in groups of three; dicots have stamens and petals in groups of four or more. Leaves in monocots have parallel veins whereas dicots have leaves arranged in a network. Monocots seldom have secondary growth (widening of stems and roots, especially in woody species) but dicots usually do.[3] There are other differences, but these are ones we can easily see and recognize. By the way, there are other monocots, ranging from orchids to lilies, palms to bananas, and asparagus to onions, but these plant families are not considered to be grasses.

All in all, about one-quarter of all plant species are monocots. Not an insignificant number, and they are major contributors to the world's biomass, not to mention sources of food for us humans as well as the rest of the animal kingdom.

So, for the purposes of this book, we have had to make some hard choices as to where to draw the line when talking about monocots, or the book would be twice as large! For us, as a definition, grasses (as an arbitrary line in the botanical sand) include those families and species that belong to the true grasses, along with rushes and sedges. We apologize to those monocots left behind (at least in this book).—JM

Form, Function, and Fit

1

They say that the prairies are grasslands. What does that mean?

Temperate grasslands are found on every continent, except for Antarctica, of course. They are typified by being found in the interior of continents and are often adjacent to mountain ranges.

Grasslands are significant biomes, as they are often massive in area, in the range of 8 percent of all of Earth's land surface.[1] Generally, grassland biomes (geographical areas with unique climate, flora, and fauna) are relatively flat. They experience moderate temperatures as well as precipitation. They have great vistas with few native trees and woodlands. The grasses that are native to the biome have huge root systems that dive deep into the soil, holding it in place and keeping erosion to a minimum. Those roots are super for accessing moisture in the subsoils and groundwater. The grasses are long-lived and support a huge diversity of other flora and wildlife species. A grassland biome maintains a soil organic matter percentage in the range of 10 to 12 percent, along with stable cycling of nutrients and biomass.

The benefits of prairie grasslands are myriad, and we need to encourage the biodiversity they support.

As a result, our Canadian grasslands have little remaining of the original native grasslands. I believe it is important to advocate for protecting the remaining undisturbed grasslands for the valuable functions they provide us all. They are so important for soil and water conservation, habitat for wildlife (especially pollinators), regulating our climate, preventing large-scale flooding, and conserving the valuable water resources that provide our drinking water and moisture for our crops.[3]

The Canadian prairies are the northern edge of the Northern Great Plains, which include both the Canadian provinces of Manitoba, Saskatchewan, and Alberta and many states of the United States of America. The Northern Great Plains were formed millions of years ago as the Rocky Mountains grew. Within the plains are three distinct groups: dry, mesic, and wet, each with its own unique flora. The mesic prairie in Canada, largely in Saskatchewan, forms the "breadbasket of Canada."[2] However, with the advent of the settling of Canada in the late 1800s and into the 1900s, along with agricultural endeavours, much of our prairie grasslands have been disturbed in order to cultivate and produce the world's wheat, oats, barley, and rye, along with other food crops.

Beyond the value of our prairies to ourselves and all the flora and fauna that inhabit them, they are magnificently beautiful. They are also our home. —JM

How do perennial and annual ornamental grasses differ?

It sounds straightforward. Annual grasses, by definition, will complete their life cycle within one growing season — literally from seed to seed in a year. Perennial grasses are those species that live for more than two years, often for many years appearing to be permanent fixtures in the landscape.

However, the perennialism of any species is dependent on several environmental factors, largely beyond our control. First and foremost is species hardiness for our climate. Many species of grasses, rushes, and sedges that are available to us originate in eastern Asia, especially China and Japan. Depending on the original native range for the species, it may or may not be hardy enough in our climate to survive our widely variable Canadian winters. If not, then for all intents and purposes, it is an annual in our world.

Many of our grasses harvested as food crops are annual in nature. Wheat, barley, oats, rice, and corn are all huge economically important grasses as food sources. In sustainable agriculture and horticulture, research work is now being done to develop the perennialization of many annual food crops to create "wide hybrid crosses."[4] The goal is to reduce annual inputs of seed, fertilizers, and pesticides toward creating sustainable and ample food supplies while repairing our depleted ecosystems.

Truly perennial species include many grasses native to the prairies, along with introductions of species whose native ranges may be as harsh as the one where our gardens are located. Given the range of the Canadian Plant Hardiness Zones across the prairies, what is perennial in southern Manitoba may very well be an annual up in northern Alberta.

Another factor in the mix is the moderation of our winters, specifically the minimum and median winter temperatures, where species that we always thought of as annuals can now survive and thrive as perennials in protected areas of our gardens. Who knows where the changing climate will take us — or rather the grass species we desire in the future? — JM

Tufted hair grass is a hardy perennial grass species on the prairies.

What is the difference between clumping and spreading grasses?

Quite a lot actually!

Clumping grasses are those that form a distinct crown or tuft. They grow in girth, taking their time about it. They are also well behaved, staying put where they are planted, only needing to be controlled by dividing them every so often. There are many species of grasses in this category, which is a great thing since these are the ones most preferred for their politeness in the garden. In this group are our well-known grasses such as the fescues (*Festuca* spp.), oat grasses (*Helictotrichon* spp.), and feather reed grasses (*Calamagrostis* spp.) but also many sedges and rushes.

On the other hand, spreading or rhizomatic grasses literally know no bounds. They are often referred to as "running grasses." The name says it all. They grow through long underground rhizomes, where each node produces a new plant. The net result is grasses that quickly develop into large patches or colonies, with no central or mother plant. Instead, they develop into dense stands with multiple stems and will travel without check.

There is a third group of grasses that are a subset of the rhizomatic group—those with short rhizomes. Into this category fall the turfgrasses, but others appear as mounds and are relatively well behaved. Think of switchgrass (*Panicum virgatum*), prairie dropseed (*Sporobolus heterolepis*), and yellow prairie grass (*Sorghastrum nutans*). All perfectly well behaved, so long as you keep your eye on them!

As you might guess, rhizomatous grasses can be invasive, and hard to control. Many are considered weeds. Just think of quack grass (*Elytrigia repens*) and shudder. But consider, too, blue lyme grass (*Leymus arenarius*) and gardener's garters, a.k.a. ribbon grass (*Phalaris arundinacea* 'Picta'), which can be most effective with a solid barrier containing it. In Calgary they have been planted in the centres of traffic circles to great effect. If you spot a species with "joint" included in its common name, you can be guaranteed it is vigorous. A terrific example is bluejoint grass (*Calamagrostis canadensis*). Others that are rhizomatous include smooth brome (*Bromus inermis*), Amur silver grass (*Miscanthus sacchariflorus*), and cogon grass (*Imperata cylindrica*).

Oat grasses, such as this variegated type, have excellent garden etiquette.

When selecting the grass species you wish to include in your garden, do research ahead of time to know just what sort of root systems your choices possess. Should there be a plant at the nursery that catches your eye and is not one you have researched, take a look at the pot. You will have a fair chance at learning what group of roots it falls into by how it presents. Look for a crown or lack thereof. If you can, take the root ball out of the pot and look at it, specifically for the telltale darning needle-like rhizomes. Then you won't have any surprises once it gets into the garden and settles into its new home.[5] — JM

What do we mean when we talk about warm-season and cool-season grasses?

Cool-season and warm-season grasses differ in the way they use carbon dioxide in the process of photosynthesis. As gardeners, we don't necessarily have to worry about understanding the fascinating chemistry involved in how plants grow. We just need to know what we're getting into when we're making our ornamental grass (or turfgrass) selections for our landscapes.

Cool-season grasses actively grow during the cooler temperatures and shorter day lengths of spring and autumn. They go dormant during the summer when temperatures soar. On the other hand, warm-season grasses relish the heat and grow the most rapidly during the late spring through early autumn. The best time to direct sow or plant cool-season grasses is in the spring or the fall, while warm-season grasses should be sown or planted in the late spring. There are both annual and perennial species in each category.

Common cool-season perennial grasses suitable for prairie gardens include blue fescue (*Festuca glauca*), blue oat grass (*Helictotrichon sempervirens*), and tufted hair grass (*Deschampsia cespitosa*). Kentucky bluegrass (*Poa pratensis*), which is a common species used in our lawns, is also a cool-season grass. Switchgrass (*Panicum virgatum*) is a common warm-season grass.[6] — SN

Blue fescue is a popular cool-season grass, with a desirable colour that makes it a standout in the garden. This cultivar is 'Sapphire'.

Blue switchgrass is a warm-season grass that is a perennial in many parts of the prairies.

What are sedges? How are they different from grasses?

Sedges (*Carex* spp.) may look a lot like grasses, but they are in a completely different family. While grasses hail from Poaceae, sedges are part of the Cyperaceae family. Telling them apart only by sight isn't easy, but if you cut a grass stem open, it will be hollow, and the sliced cross-section will be cylindrical in shape. A sedge's stem isn't hollow. The stem has three sides, which causes its cross-section to appear triangular.

Like grasses and rushes, sedges are adaptable to many types of soil conditions and live in diverse ecosystems, not just in open meadows where they are commonly associated, but in wetlands and even on the edges of forests. They can be important additions to your garden, as well, not simply because they are beautiful but also as habitat for wildlife. The seed heads are food for birds such as juncos, grouse, and ducks as they head into winter. Caterpillars of moths and butterflies also feed on the plants; many of these insects are pollinators that go on to benefit other plants in the garden. (Sedges themselves are wind pollinated and don't require insects to assist in the process.) Their densely fibrous root systems make them good candidates to plant where erosion control is needed on a slope.

Ducks are big into the sedges, rushes, and grasses that grow along the edges of wetlands!

Sedges are considered cool-season plants and, as such, will slow or halt their active growth in the heat of summer. They green up early in the spring and will quickly produce their flowers before the summer. Once the cooler temperatures of late summer and early autumn hit, they turn green again and go strong right up until the hard frosts.

Ready to grow some sedges in your prairie garden? Look for selections such as Bebb's sedge (*Carex bebbii*), Dewey's sedge (*C. deweyana*), Raynolds' sedge (*C. raynoldsii*), and Richardson's sedge (*C. richardsonii*). Source seeds from these plants at your local native plant supplier.

Just for fun, there are some other sedge relatives that you may come across in your readings or wanderings. These are not true sedges but include the so-called flatsedges, nutsedges, and umbrella sedges in the genus *Cyperus*. Some of these you definitely don't want in your garden: yellow nutsedge (*C. esculentus*), for example, is considered an invasive species in most provinces in Canada.[7] —SN

We're usually offering advice about what types of plants to grow, but yellow nutsedge is one selection we're recommending you avoid.

Are rushes grasses?

The short answer is no. They belong to the family Juncaceae and comprise a group of water-loving plants that resemble grasses. There are approximately 120 species of rushes native to North America. One way to identify a rush is to look at a cross-section of its stem, which is rounded in shape. The leaves of rushes do not sport tiny hairs (called trichomes). Rushes grow on the edges of ponds and marshes and love boggy, consistently damp areas. They will be just fine if the soil dries out periodically, as long as they receive plenty of water the rest of the time.

Rushes provide important habitat for wildlife and insects. Interesting research has been done on common rush (*Juncus effusus*), which is widespread in the United States and the southern parts of Canada. It has been discovered that the rhizomatous roots of common rush work with certain beneficial bacteria that can help filter impurities from water.

There are several species of rushes found on the prairies, including slender rush (*J. tenuis*), thread rush (*J. filiformis*), bog or moor rush (*J. stygius* var. *americanus*), and Baltic rush (*J. balticus*). You'd be hard pressed to find most of these in your local nursery, however. Instead, keep an eye open for a few notable cultivars to try instead, such as:

Corkscrew rush (*J. effusus* 'Spiralis'): The first time I saw this plant, I was smitten — it's just so unique and fun. Corkscrew rush has marvellous, twisted stems and no leaves, and it looks fabulous as the thriller part of a container. Bear in mind that it is an annual on the prairies. Giant corkscrew rush (*J. effusus* 'Big Twister') is even bigger and more boldly curly. There is a variegated type as well.

Hard rush (*J. inflexus*): This is a wonderful perennial rush (to hardiness zone 4), with upright, stiff, vividly blue-green stems and leaves. It can grow up to three feet (one metre) in height, including the flower. 'Blue Arrows' is a cultivar that is even more blue in colour, but it is considered an annual on the prairies.[8] —SN

What is scouring rush? Is it a true rush?

Scouring rush is not a true rush. It is a horsetail and more closely related to ferns than anything else. The name scouring rush comes from the fact that the plants contain silica and historically were used like scrubbers to clean surfaces, whereas field horsetail is consumed by many mammals from caribou to bears and used by Indigenous peoples for remedies for osteoporosis, bladder, and kidney ailments.

Scouring rush (*Equisetum hyemale*) and its relative field horsetail (*E. arvense*) are common denizens of the damp understoreys of forests as well as boggy areas of the prairie provinces. Equisetums have a long history on the planet and are the only genus in the plant family Equisetaceae. They first appear in the fossil record during the Carboniferous period, 325 million years ago, and they have been thriving ever since. They reproduce not by seeds, but rather by spores.[9]—SN & JM

Field horsetail is a fascinating plant that will quickly populate damp, shaded spaces.

Are ornamental grasses useful to pollinators?

Ornamental grasses, be they native or introduced species, play a vital role in our gardens for their ability to provide habitat for pollinators. Grasses are stellar at providing food, shelter, nesting sites, and larval hosts for a range of pollinating insects, birds, and mammals. Planted among our other herbaceous perennials, they can provide corridors for pollinators to move around and protection from predators such as ground beetles and spiders to boot.

Their flowers, though not as obvious to us as other, showier plants, provide loads of pollen for bees, wasps, flies, beetles, and ants. As grasses are wind pollinated, they do not produce nectar for butterflies, moths, and dragonflies, but what they do contribute is food and protection for the egg-laying and larval stages of these species. The caterpillars will attach their chrysalises to the stems and leaves, secure in the knowledge that they will not be spotted amongst the growth. The pupae will drop to the ground and snuggle into the thatch or inside the crowns of clumping grasses for warmth and protection from predators.

Those seed heads contain zillions of seeds that provide food for insects. Think of ants trundling along the soil carrying seeds back to their nests. Strictly speaking, birds are not pollinators except for hummingbirds, which are nectar lovers. But birds feast on the seeds nonetheless, keeping predators of our pollinators in check, which helps balance the ecosystem.

Bees and other nesting insect pollinators find grasses to be most hospitable for overwintering underground nesting sites, tucking themselves in at the base of the clumps. In particular, yellow prairie grass is well known for providing nesting sites, as well as being a larval host for many skipper butterflies. Those long stems and leaves are also ideal material come spring for other nests for both birds and insects.

To encourage our pollinators to take full advantage of the ornamental grasses we provide for them, do plant them in small masses or drifts. Leave a bit of room between the plants so that they can bulk up over time, but don't hugely space them apart. That will serve to create the essential corridors and protections necessary for survival. Leave the plants to shine in winter by not cutting them back come fall. Cut down, they may look neat and tidy throughout the winter months, but by doing so we have halved their value for pollinators.

I don't even remove last year's growth in the spring, allowing the new growth to come through the old. They are just as beautiful, and a natural duff layer or mulch develops, which provides manifold benefits.

While perennial ornamental plants are favoured by pollinators, annuals contribute their fair share too in terms of pollen and seed throughout the growing season, not to mention plant debris come fall. While we may need to dismantle pots and containers at the end of the season, take the time to create bundles of stems and leaves and prop or place them in the garden for winter. They will be well used and in the spring are easy to place in the compost pile.

So, yes, grasses are tremendously important for our pollinators.[10] —JM

Leave grasses intact over the winter as a benefit to many different living organisms. Plus, what a sight for sore eyes in a time of dreary cold!

How do grasses help with soil erosion?

Grasses have extensive root systems. Clumping grasses have roots that dive deep into the soil, anchoring it in place. They have dense crowns and widespread webs of fibrous roots that won't go anywhere, tenaciously hanging on in the worst of weathers. Rhizomatic grasses have a dense network of roots that exist in the topsoil and/or subsoil layers, without going so deep. Their above-ground structures are well designed to capture and direct rainfall, along with creating physical barriers that break the strength of winds.

The net result is that grasses are excellent at stabilizing soils. Their roots literally hold soils in place. Should there be an erosion event with topsoil being blown away, those leaves will capture and hang on to soil particles. Rainfall will be held on to and allowed to sink into the soil, enhancing soil moisture content. Grasses will prevent rainfall runoff, which may have the dual disadvantages of literally carrying away soil with the water before the water has a chance to infiltrate the soil. In an increasingly dry climate, whenever we get that gift from the sky, we want to hang on to all that we get!

Grasses also prevent soil compaction from heavy raindrops and hailstones, especially when augmented with a layer of mulch between the clumps.

Where grasses really shine is on hillsides, where erosion is much more of a threat. Those grasses cut the velocity of winds going down the slopes, as well as slowing the rate at which rainfall will travel, effectively preventing runnels from forming.[11] —JM

If you've ever had to dig up turfgrass to plant a tree or create a new garden space, you know exactly how back-breaking it can be to get through this dense mass of roots.

Are grasses allelopathic? What does that mean? How will they affect other plants?

Allelopathy is one of the ways that plant species create a competitive edge for themselves. Allelopathic plants produce allelochemicals that affect the growth of other plants, either by suppressing germination or increasing the rate of growth.[12] Literally these chemicals prevent other plants from effectively establishing themselves nearby and having all the resources they need to flourish. The phytotoxins can be exuded into the soil from the roots, be an airborne gas, or even leach from the plant residue as it breaks down.[13]

Black walnut (*Juglans nigra*) is often cited as being the poster child for allelopathy, as nothing will grow under or around a black walnut tree. Sunflowers are also allelopathic, as well as many weeds. Quack grass, a menace to many gardeners, is allelopathic, which is another good reason to go after it in spring and get those roots out of the beds.

There are a number of grasses that are allelopathic, including tall fescue (*Festuca arundinacea*), creeping red fescue (*F. rubra*), perennial ryegrass (*Lolium perenne*), and annual ryegrass (*L. rigidum*). Kentucky bluegrass (*Poa pratensis*), the staple species for our lawns, is also allelopathic. Go figure!

Grain crops such as wheat (*Triticum* spp.), barley (*Hordeum* spp.), and oats (*Avena* spp.) are allelopathic to some degree. Agriculture uses these crops intentionally to suppress certain weeds. Gardeners can use wheat straw in pathways to suppress weeds in troublesome areas.

Cover crops such as fall rye (*Secale cereale*) are great to suppress early germination of weeds. However, when cutting it down and integrating it into the soil, sufficient time must be given for it to decompose before sowing the season's crops or else the germination of vegetable seeds will suffer.

When integrating grasses into our beds, it is wise to observe how other plants behave around them. Should you notice certain plants edging their skirts away from the grasses, it might be wise to move either them or the grasses, so both are happier.

Wheat is much more than just gluten and carbs!

As always, nothing in nature is entirely "bad." Those allelopathic grasses are workhorses for improving soil fertility, weed suppression, and boosting soil life diversity, not to mention food production. We just need to be aware of the opportunities and challenges when including them in our gardens. —JM

How are grasses used in naturalistic garden design?

Karl Foerster, an eminent gardener and plant breeder of the twentieth century, famously described grasses as "the hair of mother earth."[14] It is such a powerful description of grasses, evoking as it does the vision of grasses swaying in the breeze in fields the world over.

In his book *Einzug der Gräser und Farne in die Gärten*, Foerster became one of the first proponents of including grasses as design elements in the garden. This seminal work described the origins and properties of grasses, along with their multiple functions in the garden. Today, he is most familiar to grass aficionados because he was honoured with his name being given to one of the most used ornamental grasses, that being 'Karl Foerster' feather reed grass (*Calamagrostis* × *acutiflora* 'Karl Foerster').

Naturalistic garden design, which has come into prominence through the work of Doug Tallamy, Piet Oudolf, Nigel Dunnett, Ian Hodgson, and Noel Kingsbury, among many others, follows in the footsteps of Karl Foerster. These designers and authors have taken the use of grasses in the garden to new levels. The result is the naturalistic garden design movement, which "combines a gardener's needs and desires with nature's dictates; its design cannot be premeditated because its inherent beauty is inextricably linked to the landscape on which it is created."[15]

Naturalistic garden design looks to work with nature and not against it, using scientific and garden design principles to create gardens that have a unique beauty and appeal, matched with the concerns for the environment in the twenty-first century.

The goals of naturalistic garden design are to not only conserve but also increase biodiversity, regenerate our soils, and give back to nature. The movement embraces an organic approach, where the seasonality of the cycles of birth and decay is embraced, where nothing is static and everything evolves as the seasons pass. There is an emphasis on plant forms and structure, rather than colour and flowers. The gardener "seeks to minimize typical garden inputs like pesticides, herbicides, and fertilizers, while recycling its outputs from rainwater to garden waste, all in the name of self-sustainability."[16]

Grasses have important roles in naturalistic garden design. Think of the grasslands, our prairies. Before agricultural disturbance and urban construction, the grasslands were a stable and sustaining environment. Grasses are a structural layer in these designs. They are the basis upon which designed plant communities evolve, as they are sociable plants. Grasses love being in close proximity to themselves and other species. They are good neighbours or companion plants. Perennial grasses in such a design are building blocks, providing continuity over the seasons, as well as colours ranging from the greens, yellows, whites, and, yes, pinks of spring and early summer onward through the colour palette of tans, browns, bronzes, oranges, reds, and purples of fall and lingering into winter when their golden and tan hues shine through the snow. Grasses provide textures and shapes. They are linear monocots rather than branching plants, like dicots, providing elegance along with feathery texture and strong forms. Grasses provide movement, repetition, and sound. Depending on the movement of air, they whisper or rustle or even rattle in a good stiff breeze. They provide lightness, relying on multiple stems as a statement of their presence, rather than bulky forms. They can be almost transparent or provide screening and a degree of privacy.

So let us include grasses within the visions and goals we have for our gardens. Like the grassland biome that is our prairies, they can define us and sustain us. They are truly the "hair of mother earth." —JM

No, this is not a garden, but think of the inspiration you can draw from the combination of native grasses and wildflowers in this scene!

From the Ground Up—Planting and Caring for Your Ornamental Grasses

2

Do I need to stratify the seeds of perennial ornamental grasses before I sow them? How do I do this?

Stratifying seeds is a technique to break dormancy inhibiters by subjecting seeds to a cold period prior to sowing them. Species that originated in the northern temperate climates typically need this process to break dormancy. It makes sense; they come from areas that get winter for at least some of the months prior to spring arriving. Plants are smart. Why would they want seeds that self-sow in the fall to germinate just as winter arrives?

It is our cool-season grasses that require stratification before sowing. Those that are warm-season grasses mostly come from the tropics or the southern hemisphere. They never developed this germination inhibition, so they can go straight from the seed packet into the ground or seedling tray.

Cool-season grasses can be sown outside in the fall, where the conditions for germination will be met over the winter months should you live in an area where winter comes regularly and stays and stays (sigh). Or you can stratify them using one of two methods:

The first method is dry stratification, which is suitable for most grasses. Simply place the seed in a protective container such as a baggie or plastic container. Put the container in the refrigerator for at least two months to upwards of six months, depending on the species. Or if you have an unheated garage attached to the house, they can go in there, up next to the house wall so that they don't thoroughly freeze.

Moist stratification is more appropriate for species originating from wetter areas such as wetlands or marshes, especially sedges and rushes. In this method, place a moistened material such as peat, coir fibre, vermiculite, or sand in a container. Mix in the seed and store it in the fridge or an unheated garage for the required length of time.

Both methods will result in grass species having much better germination and initial growth rates.[1] —JM

The seeds of wild grasses will naturally stratify over winter.

What type of growing medium do ornamental grasses need when grown in containers?

We recommend a growing mix of one part topsoil, one part compost, and one part coir or peat moss, with a handful of perlite or pumice added for good measure (and to boost the texture and structure of your growing medium). It's that easy! Most grasses don't need rich soil, so adding more topsoil than compost is quite all right. This isn't the kind of recipe that you can easily fail at. —SN

Grasses are easy-care solutions for containers. Even though they don't have colourful flowers, they offer a unique beauty and texture that can enhance the landscape.

Can ornamental grasses tolerate clay soil? In what types of soil do grasses grow best?

Ornamental grasses are versatile. For the most part, they have adapted to the full range of soils across the prairies, with at least a few grasses growing well in each soil type. Many will do well outside their preferred soil type as well.

Generally, you will be successful establishing most species if you have well-draining, moisture-retentive soils with decent fertility.

The trick is to know as much as possible about the species you want to grow, with particular attention to its native range and habitats. Those that are found anchoring sand dunes are the least likely to enjoy full-on damp, heavy clay soils.

Those that like sandy, light soils include the fountain grasses (*Pennisetum* spp.), switchgrasses (*Panicum* spp.), silver grasses (*Miscanthus* spp.), hair grasses (*Deschampsia* spp.), feather grasses (*Stipa* spp.), and feather reed grasses (*Calamagrostis* spp.) along with a variety of sedges, oat grasses (*Helictotrichon* spp.), and some fescues (*Festuca* spp.) Those genera are a large slice of the perennial ornamental grasses we see in nurseries.

So, what grasses enjoy the heavier, more moisture-retentive, clay soils? Look no further than the vast majority of species that make their home on the prairies and northern plains. The bluestem grasses (*Schizachyrium* spp.), dropseed grasses (*Sporobolus* spp.), and grama grasses (*Bouteloua* spp.) are all known for handling these soils well, along with fescues and many more.

But here comes the versatility of grasses. Switchgrass and fountain grasses also thrive in clay soils. In fact, so long as you amend clay soils with plenty of compost to lighten them up a bit, along with improving drainage, and site them carefully, you can usually be assured of success with most grasses.[2] —JM

Grama grass has it all: dark blue flowers, striking cream-coloured seed heads, a slow, rhizomatous spread—and as a bonus, it can handle clay soils.

Do ornamental grasses need a certain pH for optimal growth?

As with most of the perennial and annual plants we grow, the ideal soil pH factor is slightly acidic, in the range of 5 to 7.[3] However, most of the ornamental grasses that we grow are fairly flexible as to pH, especially if the soil is well buffered by lots of organic matter.

As always, consider the native range for the grasses you choose to grow. The typical soil for that region gives you a good sense of what the plants prefer, and if the soil is highly acidic, then you may wish to forgo that one in favour of others. Incidentally, the grass that we grow as lawns prefers a pH of around 5, which might explain why some of our lawns struggle as they cannot absorb the nutrients provided by fertilizers very well, given our soils generally are alkaline with a pH of 7 or higher.[4]

Grass species native to the prairies have adapted to the alkaline conditions that prevail in most of our gardens. But there are others that do well in higher-pH soils too, from fountain grasses to moor grasses and onward to blue oat grass and more. —JM

Variegated moor grass is somewhat more tolerant of higher-pH soils than other grasses.

I bought some ornamental grasses in the spring. Do I need to harden them off before planting them outside?

To increase your chances of success with your new grasses, the answer is: absolutely! As with your other plants, the transition from being inside a greenhouse or inside a store to the harsher, most likely chillier and windier outdoors can be shocking. To combat this, take your containers of grasses outdoors each day for a few hours. Place the containers in a sheltered spot, out of conditions such as the hot sun and desiccating wind. Bring the containers indoors at night. Over a period of one to two weeks, gradually increase the number of hours you leave the plants outdoors. At the end of the hardening-off period—and if the weather forecast isn't showing any more freezing temperatures—you can keep the grasses outside, where they can be transplanted into bigger containers or into the ground. —SN

This 'Golden Dew' tufted hair grass is a new purchase from a garden centre. Be sure to harden off your plant purchases before transplanting them into their new home.

What is the proper way to plant container-grown ornamental grasses into the ground?

One of the big things to remember when planting ornamental grasses is that most of them are not particularly choosy when it comes to their nutrient needs. In fact, many prefer soil on the lean side, and they are adaptable to a wide range of soil textures as well. That means you should not amend the soil you are planting them in.

To plant grass grown in a container, dig a hole as deep as the container and at least twice the width. Keep the backfill as you'll need it later.

Carefully remove the plant from the pot. If this isn't an easy task due to the tightness of the roots in the container, use a pair of scissors to cut away the pot. (It's much better to do this than yank up the grass by the leaves and stems and risk damaging it.)

Once the grass is freed from the container, loosen the roots with your hands. This will help the plant roots spread once the grass is in the ground.

Place the grass into the hole and surround it with the backfill. Don't bury the plant deeper than the depth it was at when it was in the container. Hold the stems and leaves upright (you may need a friend to help you out) while you're backfilling so that the leaves and stems are not buried in the soil. Gently tamp down the soil around the plant.

Now—just add water![5]—SN

Should I mulch my perennial ornamental grasses? What types of mulch are suitable?

Mulching around our ornamental grasses is as much a necessity as with other herbaceous perennials. Not only does mulch protect the soil from moisture loss and erosion, but it deters weeds from germinating. The one thing you really don't need with grasses are weeds growing into the clumps, especially rhizomatous weeds, as they are the very devil to get out!

In a natural grassland the mulch generally consists of the plant debris from previous years, which creates a duff layer that protects the soil. Laying down last year's stems and leaves, either chopped up or whole, in between the plants will serve to mimic that natural mulch that most grasses prefer. Over time, as you add successive layers with each season's materials, a lovely layer will accumulate and will slowly be absorbed into the soil, enriching the nutrients, improving the texture, and encouraging soil life biodiversity.

Alternatively, a layer of approximately 1 to 2 inches (2.5 to 5 centimetres) of a fine montane or wood chip mulch serves the same purpose. Montane mulch, essentially a fine mix of conifer needles and bark, will break down faster than wood chips. —JM

Some inspiration for your garden! Take a look at this self-produced mulch in a natural grassland.

What should I use for fertilizer for my perennial ornamental grasses? When should I apply it?

Our ornamental grasses need very little in the way of fertilizer. They evolved for the most part in areas with soils on the lean side. Indeed, because they primarily focus on growing foliage, without the need to develop showy flowers or seed heads, they seldom need the amount of additional nutrients that other herbaceous perennials require.

Once established, usually after the second year, all that is usually needed is some compost spread around the crowns on an annual basis in spring when growth resumes. These nutrients will assist in developing extensive root systems, and, in the case of clumping grasses, will both increase their girth and help in producing more seed heads. Rhizomatous grasses won't even need that assist.

A sure sign that grasses are receiving too many nutrients, either from the rich soil we create in our gardens or from applied fertilizers, is excessive and lush growth that often flops over. Grasses are born to be on a lean diet.

Should your grasses be exhibiting signs of stress, such as yellowing leaves or dull, faded colours, then a little TLC in the way of a slow-release granular fertilizer high in nitrogen might be warranted. But do eliminate other potential causes of stress such as overwatering, underwatering, or pests and diseases. Fertilizing as a course of action should be the last choice, as you may just make the problem worse.[6] —JM

How often should I fertilize my annual ornamental grasses? What type of fertilizer should I use?

You can go easy on fertilizer for all ornamental grasses, even annual ones, which means the gardener can pretty much just sit back and relax after ensuring some compost is incorporated into the growing medium of grass plants in containers or garden beds. Compost is an amendment rather than a fertilizer (as we don't know the specific breakdown of measurable ingredients in compost), but the slow release of the nutrients it contains will benefit annual grasses over the growing season. You don't want to overfertilize your grasses: not only can too much fertilizer (in particular, nitrogen) attract insect pests to the fresh succulent plant parts, but it can cause leaves and stems to flop around and look unsightly.

If you are growing annual ornamental grasses in beds or in ground, you can simply side-dress them with a layer of approximately ½ inch (1.2 centimetres) of compost in the spring. There is no need to till the compost into the soil. Just sprinkle it around the base of the plants. Soil micro-organisms and wind and water will help work it into the soil and get it to the plant roots.

If you are planting your annual grasses in containers, incorporate some compost into your growing medium. Our suggested recipe for growing medium is on page 34, but a general recommendation is that up to one-third of your mix should be composed of compost. The nutrients in the compost will be slowly released over the growing season and you shouldn't have to add extra. — SN

How do I know when it's time to water my ornamental grasses? How much water should I apply?

Like many other plants, ornamental grasses will usually wilt when they are thirsty. Prolonged lack of water may cause the foliage to turn yellow. Whether they are growing in containers, in raised beds, or in ground, the best way to tell if your grasses need a drink is to do the knuckle test. Sink your index finger into the soil up to the second knuckle. If the soil feels dry and crumbly, and you don't notice any moisture, it's time to water. If you are growing grasses in containers and you notice that you must frequently water, it's time to check the roots as the plants may be root-bound and need to be transplanted into a larger container or divided (see pages 44–45), then repotted.

In the first year after they have been planted, perennial ornamental grasses should be watered regularly and thoroughly to help them establish their roots. This may mean you have to haul out the watering can at least two times a week, perhaps more if the weather is hot and the grasses are planted in full sun. If your turfgrass has been freshly seeded, the young seedlings will need watering nearly every day as they build their root systems. When you water seedlings, take care not to drown them; they haven't yet established strong roots, so they can be easily overwhelmed with too much water and may then rot.

Established ornamental grasses planted in ground or in raised beds typically need about 1 inch (2.5 centimetres) of water each week. If it has rained, you may not need to water. The way that grasses are spaced in the garden will alter their watering needs: plants that are growing close together may need more watering than those that are spaced more widely apart. Dense, clumping grasses may also need more watering than grasses that are looser and upright.

Container-grown grasses may dry out faster than those grown in ground or in raised beds, especially in hot and windy conditions. Do that knuckle test every other day to ensure that you aren't subjecting your grasses to drought stress. Ensure your containers have excellent drainage to discourage root rot.

Know the individual needs of your annual and perennial grasses. Plant them in appropriate locations to begin with. A grass that prefers moist, partly shaded conditions will not fare as well in hot sun and will require more supplemental irrigation. Choosing the best home for your plant will be healthier for it in the long run. — SN

While you're using the watering can, practise a bit of Integrated Pest Management and inspect your ornamental grasses for any issues such as rust infections or pest insects.

How can I divide perennial ornamental grasses? When is the best time of year to do this?

One of the best and simplest ways to propagate our perennial grasses is through division. Fibrous-rooted, clumping, and bunching species, as well as rhizomatous-rooted ones, take readily to being divided and you soon will have many transplants to tuck back into the garden or share with others.

The best time to divide grasses is in the spring as soon as the ground has thawed and dried out. I often wait for just a bit of new growth to be showing before tackling the job with my spade and cleaver in hand. Best not to wait too long after that first growth. Too much new growth means that the plant will be wanting to spend most of its energy on top growth and not on re-establishing roots. You also want to avoid being too late to the game, with the heat of the summer coming on quickly, when new divisions will struggle as they try to settle into their new homes. It's sort of a Goldilocks timing for us and the plant. If you miss that window or our wonky, variable climate rushes in summer too fast for you and the plant, then wait till the fall. It's still a game of when to get the job done though. You want to wait for the summer heat to be gone, but not too late because once winter comes, it will be challenging for the plant's roots to get settled in. The best part is that, whether it's summer or fall, grasses are easygoing as to when they get divided.

On the whole, grasses will let us know when they should be divided. Over time, a grass clump will die out in the middle of the crown, and there will be vigorous growth around it. Rhizomatous grasses will be straining at the seams, with too many roots for the space allocated to them. Loss of vigorous growth with plants becoming shorter, dying back earlier in the fall, or being slow to emerge in the spring are all good indicators that they want your attention. Typically, you can plan for division every two to four years, depending on the species and growing conditions. Wait too much longer and those roots will be massive, and it will be a major operation. On the other hand, don't divide plants too frequently. Do so only after plants have a nice bulk and are well established. If divided too frequently, grasses will let you know with failed growth and by looking rather desperate and generally unhappy.

The best way to divide grass is to water the plant well a few days before the operation. A well-hydrated plant will survive the procedure much easier. Then lay down a tarp nearby. Using a sharp, curved spade or shovel, dig out the entire plant and heft it onto the tarp. Do make sure to take all of the root ball and as much of the fine roots as you can manage. Once the plant is on the tarp, natural dividing sections will be apparent. Using a sharp knife (I use a kitchen cleaver), cut the plant into those sections. Discard any parts of the plant that are dead or exhibiting diminished growth. Then immediately replant the sections back into your garden, and if any are to go elsewhere, pot them up quickly. When placing the divisions into new holes in your garden, use the existing soil but add a layer of compost on top that will protect the roots and slowly provide added nutrients as the plant re-establishes itself. Do water well, but not to the point of drowning the divisions. Then monitor them for signs of stress and to ensure that the soil remains moist but not wet. Soon they will be well on their way to becoming vigorous plants. —JM

It's much easier to divide perennial grasses when they are just popping up in the spring. This beautiful clump of 'Karl Foerster' feather reed grass may be too stressed by a summer division—plus, you might miss out on the show it puts on with its decorative flowers and seed heads!

How can I save the seed from ornamental grasses?

The key to collecting seed from your ornamental grasses is timing. It's truly everything. The seed should be dry. That means they are usually brown or tan in colour. Green seeds contain too much moisture and may rot in storage; on top of that, the embryos they contain may not yet be fully developed, which leads to seed that is not viable. Below the seed head, some of the stem should be dry as well—if the stem is still fully green, it's usually an indicator that you should wait a bit longer. Bear in mind that if you wait too long to harvest the seed, shattering may occur—the ripe, dry seed heads will burst, and the seed will fall to the ground.

When preparing grass seed for storage, you'll need to separate the chaff (husks and plant debris) from the seed. This is called threshing, and it will require some physical effort on your part. There isn't one way to successfully thresh—explore various methods to determine which one is best for you. Cut the grass down by two-thirds. Stack and bundle the stalks, binding them with twine. Place the stalks into an old pillowcase with the seed heads inside. Cinch the opening of the case closed, holding the grasses by their stalks. Then beat the grasses inside the pillowcase against a floor. The seed will dislodge from the heads. Another way to do this is to use a large, clean garbage can. Bundle the grasses and beat them against the sides of the interior of the can. The seeds will fall into the bottom of the can.

Once you have separated the seed, it's time to winnow. Winnowing will separate the smaller particles of chaff from the seed. You can use a screen or wire mesh sieve to winnow. Rub the pieces of seed heads against the screen and sort the plant debris from the seed. It is a time-consuming process, but you'll be thankful when it comes time to sow the seed next year. (And if you are eating the seed, threshing and winnowing are absolutely necessary!)

Store dried grass seed in glassine or paper envelopes, or in glass or plastic jars with lids. The seed may be kept at room temperature and should remain viable for several years, depending on the species. —SN

Should I cut back my perennial grasses before winter sets in?

You can, if you wish — it's not going to hurt anything. But there are huge benefits to cutting them back in the spring instead. Not only do the seed heads of many grasses look stunning against a dreary winter landscape, but keeping the dried stems and foliage in place traps snow that serves to insulate the plant roots and protects them from temperature fluctuations. As well, the seed heads from many ornamental grasses provide food for birds and wildlife at a time when pickings are slim.

If you choose to cut back your perennial grasses in the fall, trim them down by approximately two-thirds, leaving one-third of the plants above ground. If you wait until the spring, shear the dry stalks away just as the fresh new growth is emerging from the base of the plant. Waiting too long makes the job more difficult. — SN

This 'Karl Foerster' feather reed grass was cut down in the previous fall and the new growth is emerging in the spring.

Can I use grasses as a fall cover crop?

Grasses make a terrific fall-sown cover crop. Come spring, you can till them into the soil as a green manure.

Such green manures provide a multitude of benefits at a fairly low cost, much less than many other soil amendments and fertilizers. To start with, the growth in the fall can protect the soil over the winter, especially in areas with variable snow cover. Between desiccating winds stripping out soil moisture and freeze-and-thaw cycles when soils warm up only to go back into the deep-freeze again, plus the potential for soil to literally blow away in the winter, the cover provided by quickly establishing fine, fibrous root systems and top growth left in place is a top-notch conservation measure. Once cultivated into the soil, the biomass of the crop will contribute to an improved soil texture, nutrient base, infiltration rate of moisture, and buffered pH values, not to mention increased soil life biodiversity. It is the best way I know to improve organic matter content in soils regeneratively and sustain soil life over the winter, all with the least amount of work!

There are two main groups of fall-sown cover crops. One is cool-season grasses, which are sown at the tail end of the summer. They quickly germinate and produce top growth that is killed by the winter temperatures but leaves lots of "green manure" to degrade into the soil, contributing nitrogen and organic matter. This group does not require tilling in the spring to terminate growth and allows for an earlier sowing of other seed in the space. Ideal candidates include common oat (*Avena sativa*), common wheat (*Triticum* spp.), and winter triticale (× *Triticosecale* 'Wittmack'), a hybrid of wheat and rye.

The other group of cover crops can survive our winters and resume growth in the spring. It is best to sow the cover crop around the middle of August, so that it has a chance to germinate, develop good roots, and produce some nice top growth before winter causes it to go dormant above the crown. Growth resumes as soon as soil conditions permit. Then, once the growth reaches some six inches (fifteen centimetres), it is cultivated into the soil in mid-spring, creating that excellent biomass. Alternatively, it can be sown at the end of the fall once the potential for germination has passed, and it will overwinter and sprout in the spring as soon as conditions are there for germination.

Bar none, fall rye (*Secale cereale*), known also as winter rye, is the hardiest of fall-sown cover crops on the prairies. Do make sure your purchase is labelled with the botanical name, so that you do not mistakenly sow *Lolium multiflorum*, which is sometimes called Italian ryegrass and used for lawns. Also, you do not want to sow the perennial species *L. perenne*, which may be called just ryegrass.

You can often see fall rye growing in the prairies from mid-March to early April. But beware: fall rye does have allelopathic qualities, so it must be at least three weeks after it is cultivated into the soil before any other seeds can be sown in that space. My current practice is to sow fall rye in one half of a bed and plan to transplant seedlings of warm-season crops where it has been cultivated later on in the spring, just so I get lots of time for that biomass to degrade in the soil before I plant.

Alternatives to fall rye include winter wheat (*Triticum aestivum*), which is not quite as hardy but has the bonus of not being difficult to terminate come spring. Common barley (*Hordeum vulgare*) is not as reliable as fall rye, but it tolerates late-season drought and low snow cover.

The benefits of growing cover crops as green manure cannot be overstated. I encourage everyone to take the plunge![7] —JM

Want a huge boost for your garden soil? Sow a cover crop such as fall rye!

Let's Talk Lawns!

3

What are the best turfgrass species for the prairies?

If you look at the ingredients list of most of the turfgrass mixes available commercially, you're going to find that most experts recommend a mix of Kentucky bluegrass (*Poa pratensis*), perennial rye grass (*Lolium perenne*), and perhaps creeping red fescue (*Festuca rubra*), in varying amounts according to the volume of traffic on your lawn and the amount of sunlight it receives. There is nothing seriously wrong with these mixes, but I'm going to mess with the tried and the true and recommend something a little bit better, and more suitable for the prairie climate. Kentucky bluegrass and perennial ryegrass are beautiful but they're not as drought tolerant as maybe we would wish, and they will go dormant very quickly in the heat of mid-summer. To keep them looking lush, we need to invest in a huge input of water—and given the hit to the pocketbook as well as the environment, they're not the best options.

A good alternative is sheep's fescue (also known as sheep fescue, *Festuca ovina*). This is a soft, densely clumping, finely leaved turfgrass that spreads by seed, not by rhizomes as many other grasses do. It usually reaches a maximum height of only eight inches (twenty centimetres) and grows extremely slowly, so you can rest up the mower (and cross the job off your honey-do list) for most of the summer. Another bonus is sheep's fescue performs well in both sun and shade conditions, and it can tolerate a fair amount of foot traffic.[1] —SN

When is the best time to sow turfgrass seed?

Most grass seed will not germinate until the soil temperature hits 62°F (17°C) or higher, so for quick results, seed at the appropriate time during the growing season. Dormant seeding is when you sow grass seed in late autumn, just before freeze-up, to try to get a head start on germination as soon as conditions are optimal the following spring. The catch with dormant seeding is timing—if you sow too early in the fall, the seed will germinate and will not be ready for the onslaught of winter.[2] —SN

What are "eco-lawn" seed mixes?

An eco-lawn is one that stays green all season, requires no fertilizer, much less water, and little mowing. There are various mixes available, some of which contain up to six species of fescue. Other alternatives are a mix of fescues, clover, and other native grasses along with other broadleaf species. What eco-lawn mixes do not contain are Kentucky bluegrass (*Poa pratensis*) and perennial ryegrass seed (*Lolium perenne*).—JM

What is the purpose of power raking and aerating? Are they necessary for a healthy lawn?

Come spring, there is often a knock on the door, and someone is there offering to power rake and/or aerate your lawn. It sounds like a good idea. But is it?

Lawns often take a beating over the course of a season. Heavily trafficked areas may become compacted, impacting the ability of water and fertilizers to get down into the root zone. The soil underneath may be in layers if the lawn was laid down as sod, and roots can have a hard time getting into the subsoil layer.

Lawns naturally have a thatch layer, composed of grass clippings, old stems, and roots along with debris that drifts in. Thatch is good for lawns. It helps insulate the root zone from our variable temperatures, slows moisture loss, and helps capture moisture, directing it to the roots. It also deters weed seeds from germinating. It even becomes a cushion of sorts that protects the lawn from compacting. The thatch slowly decomposes over time. However, at times the thatch can accumulate upwards of 1 inch (2.5 centimetres), too thick for its own good. Roots may grow up into it and because they are not in the soil, they are not drought tolerant. Moisture and nutrients get trapped in the thatch and do not reach the root zone. A too-thick layer of thatch encourages insect pests and pathogens to take up residence.

Enter in aerating and power raking. They are separate services and are meant to assist in rejuvenating distressed lawns or maintaining healthy ones.

Aerating involves using a machine with hollow metal tubes that extract cores of sod about 3 inches (7.5 centimetres) long from the lawn. The space the plugs leave behind allows roots to be stimulated and provides entry points for water and nutrients. Over the season the grass will fill in the holes, reinvigorating the lawn. You can leave the plugs on the lawn, and they will break down naturally to feed the soil. Or you can rake them up and compost them as it does look a bit unsightly to have the plugs lying everywhere on the lawn. (By the way, the old-fashioned way to aerate lawns was with a garden fork, literally poking holes in the sod to get the same result.) Do water the lawn thoroughly a couple of days ahead of aerating as the plugs will come out much easier and the lawn will respond to the treatment faster. Aim to fertilize a couple of days afterward for maximum benefit.

On the other hand, power raking is meant to reduce the thatch layer. A powerful mechanical rake is employed to vigorously rake out the thatch. You then rake it up and compost the debris. De-thatching can be done the old-fashioned way as well, with a regular rake. It used to be my job as a teenager to rake out the thatch. I swear I still have the calluses I built up on my hands to this day!

Power raking is very hard on grass, and the lawn will look rather beat up afterward. Do water the lawn well afterward to give it some TLC.

Should you choose to aerate or power rake, spring is a good time as the grass is coming out of dormancy. But don't do it too soon. If the soil is still frozen and/ or the grass is wet from snowmelt, then both processes will do more harm than good. Wait till the lawn is dry and new growth is beginning. Spring is also a good time for overseeding, if the grass is sparse, after either procedure. Be aware that weed seeds are also wanting to germinate in the spring. An aerated or power raked lawn provides lots of opportunities for them to grow, too.

A better time is in the early fall. Grass often begins another cycle of growth with the cooler temperatures. Should you choose to do it at this time, then complete the beautifying procedure by adding a layer of compost and raking it in.

Aerating and power raking do not need to be done every year, if at all. Power raking and aerating can be minimized if you apply compost to the lawn throughout the season and lightly rake it in. The compost will stimulate biological activity and the thatch will decompose faster, resulting in improved soil texture and less compaction. If you take care of the soil below the grass, then it will take of everything else.[3]—JM

This lawn greened up quickly after aeration and a good watering schedule.

Knock that thick thatch back for a healthier lawn.

What type of lawn fertilizer should I use in the autumn?

Don't freak out when I say that applying a nitrogen-based fertilizer is totally okay in the autumn. I know, I know—it doesn't make sense. Who wants to encourage a bunch of lush, upper green growth before the lawn is supposed to go into dormancy in anticipation of winter? The truth is that through the process of photosynthesis, nitrogen fertilizer can actually help stockpile the number of sugars found in the crown of the grass (the place where the base of the stem meets the soil). The whole thing works because grass can still take up nitrogen in the roots even when the weather has turned chilly and active top growth has slowed or even stopped. The sugars are hugely important in keeping grass from becoming damaged by freezing. As a delightful bonus, they can also help your lawn get a leg up on fresh new growth the following spring and eliminate the need for a pesky fertilizer application when you've got better things to do like enjoying the snowdrops and crocuses that are popping up.

Now, here's the clincher: the biggest problem with fertilizer application in the fall is timing it accurately. If you fertilize too early, the grass will shoot up with fresh, tender growth that will be easily harmed by freezing. The goal is to wait until approximately three weeks before freeze-up, around the second week of October in most parts of the prairies. Fertilize at half the recommended rate on the fertilizer bag (you don't need to go full rate for the fall) and always use a broadcast spreader for best results.

If you miss the window of opportunity for application, don't fret. It's better not to bother fertilizing at all than to risk timing it incorrectly and causing harm to your lawn.[4]—SN

What are the best practices for fertilizing the lawn in spring?

If you've fertilized properly in the fall, you may not actually need to fertilize in early spring, especially if you have an established lawn. If you weren't able to fertilize during the previous autumn, the fertilizer blend to use in the spring is commonly called a "turf starter." It should be slow release and have a higher percentage of phosphorus (the middle number on the fertilizer bag) to promote root development. Once the grass has completely greened up and you've mowed once or twice, you can switch to a high-nitrogen fertilizer (the first number on the bag). Bear in mind that most established lawns don't need a lot of phosphorus, so if you get sidetracked by life and miss the turf starter application in early spring, it's not really a big deal. Indeed, there are some concerns that the leaching of excess phosphates from fertilizer use can cause problems such as algae blooms in waterways.

Always use a broadcast spreader to apply fertilizer. Unless you are really good at it, scattering fertilizer by hand will lead to uneven results. Work the spreader in a north-south orientation, followed by east-west, to ensure the best coverage.[5] —SN

How do I lay sod?

First, prepare the area. Make sure the soil is on a level grade and raked free of debris. Weeds must be pulled. If you wish to lay sod overtop existing turf, make sure the lawn is mowed short and grass clippings are removed. Add two to four inches (five to ten centimetres) of topsoil mixed with compost (in a 2:1 ratio) to use as a base. Remember that grade is extremely important. This is the time to correct any issues you may have had with an uneven lawn. Think about where your walkways, patios, and driveways are and make sure your soil surfaces are located just below them. You don't want the transition between lawn and these hardscaped areas to be awkward.

Measure the area carefully and double-check your work. Don't order more sod than you need. While you're waiting for delivery, water your soil very well, ideally twenty-four to forty-eight hours before installation.

When your sod is delivered, do not let it sit, especially if it is a hot day. (I recommend trying to time delivery for when temperatures are cooler.) I worked in a garden centre for many years and if we didn't remove sod from a pallet quickly enough in the summer sun, it would begin to smoulder. It takes only a couple of hours for it to send up plumes of smoke! If you can't get to it right away, unstack the pallet to allow for air circulation. Do not wait more than twelve hours after delivery to lay sod. It's best to do the task within half that time.

Laying sod is a bit like laying a laminate floor. Lay the strips straight and line the joints up snugly. Do not overlap the pieces or things will get lumpy pretty quickly. When you start on a new row, stagger the joints as if you were constructing a brick wall. Use a sharp carpet knife to cut edges. Never tear them. The flat of the knife blade works well to press down on the joints to seal them together. Sprinkle a bit of topsoil/compost mix into the seams as you create each one.

Try not to walk or kneel on the newly laid sod as you are working, and if you accidentally compact the soil you are laying the sod onto with your feet or equipment, rake the soil again.

Reserve small cut pieces of sod for the middle of the area you're working in. If you lay small pieces on the edges, they are more likely to dry out and possibly die. The edges should be covered with full-sized pieces.

Roll the sod after you've laid it. You can rent sod rollers from businesses that offer tool rentals, and the company you purchased the sod from may also have them available. Rolling the sod helps ensure the roots of the grass are directly in contact with the topsoil/compost blend and eliminates air pockets that may pop up.

The key to success with sod is to water it immediately. Don't even wait until you've installed all of it. Lay a few pieces, then roll them, then water. Continue as you go along.

After you've laid the new sod, keep it watered deeply. The grass will take a few weeks to establish. Do not fertilize for at least a month after laying it, and do not mow it for a minimum of ten days. When you mow it for the first time, do not cut it short. Keep the grass at a length of about 3 inches (7.5 centimetres). Do not walk on the new lawn during that time either, to reduce the risk of compaction. — **SN**

Laying sod can be a labour-intensive task, but if it is cared for properly, you'll quickly be rewarded with a beautiful lawn.

What is the proper way to mow the lawn so it looks its best?

The way a lawn is mowed can have a significant effect on its growth. Following these guidelines will contribute to an attractive, well-groomed lawn.

* Mow when the weather is cool. Mowing in the heat of the day will stress the lawn. If there is a prolonged hot, dry spell, reduce the frequency of mowing, and adjust the height of your mower's blades so that the grass is not cropped as short as you usually favour.

* Make sure the lawn is dry before you mow it. Mower blades cannot make a properly sharp cut into wet grass; it will tend to clump and tear.

* Make sure your mower blades are sharp. Mower blades that are not in tip-top condition are no different than dull pruning shears that will make a poor cut in a tree branch: there is the potential to leave wounds encouraging pests and diseases.

* Each time you mow, alternate the direction you cut. Try east-west one time, then north-south, and repeat during the entire growing season. With this treatment, your turf will stand a bit more upright.

* If you can, leave your grass clippings on the lawn. (If your mower leaves clumpy swaths, you should compost the clippings instead, as thick mounds of decaying grass can encourage mould and other problems.)—SN

My dogs have made a mess of my lawn. How do I fix grass that has been damaged by urine?

We may love our pooches but our turfgrass certainly doesn't.

Dog urine contains a concentrated amount of ammonia, which can dehydrate and burn your lawn. The excess salts from accidental fertilizer spills can do the same thing. In the case of a fertilizer spill, scoop up as much of the granules as you can and safely dispose of them. For either type of damage, water the affected area deeply, then top-dress with a 1-inch (2.5-centimetre) layer of a mixture of one part loam, one part compost, and one part peat moss or coir. Then thickly apply grass seed. Gently tamp the seed down so it has contact with the soil and water it. Keep the moisture levels consistent as the seed germinates and establishes itself. Unfortunately, dog ownership will necessitate a repeat performance of this lawn repair technique...probably on an annual basis! —SN

Is artificial turf a good thing to install?

It is tempting to rip out your lawn at times, considering all the work it takes to maintain it. There is no doubt that all that watering, fertilizing, and mowing takes up time, energy, and resources. But before you do so, consider that your lawn absorbs a ton of rainfall and carbon dioxide. It supports soil life from worms to microbes and helps cool our heating world. On the other hand, artificial grass really is artificial, and green only in colour. It contributes to pollution when being manufactured and destroys the soil underneath when laid down. It provides nothing for our wildlife but accumulates all sorts of debris from animal urine and feces, dust, and so on, requiring that it be regularly washed. It also slowly fades in colour and breaks down, needing to be replaced every ten years or so, and ends up in the landfill as it is not biodegradable.

We strongly recommend you do not go there! —JM

I have a ton of weeds in my lawn. Is there anything I can do about them?

The job of weeds is to populate areas where there are disturbed or degraded soils or where the vegetation cover has been depleted or is gone. They work to improve soil structure, texture, and nutrient values. Once they have done that, their place in the scheme of things is finished and other plants take over, from ground covers and herbaceous perennials to shrubs and trees.

The problem with gardens, including lawns, is that we are always disturbing the soil and plants, striving to keep the natural order of succession from progressing. So, the weeds keep coming and we keep tearing our hair out and reaching for the tool to dig them out or the herbicide to eradicate them.

A better way is to let them do their job and move on. Or to create the conditions where there is no need for them to be there in the first place.

Starting from the root zone on up, do improve the underlying soil by regularly raking in a layer of compost overtop the grass. Over time it will increase soil texture and nutrients. All that biological activity will stimulate lots of new root growth, too. No need for those pioneering species if the soil is continually being improved.

Sparse lawns are begging for weed seed to come join in the fun. Over-sow the grass with extra seed to increase the density of the grass. If weed seeds cannot find space to land, then they won't germinate.

Mow less frequently, allowing the grass to grow longer, which also prevents weed seed from landing. Set the blades higher so the grass is always a little longer, which will prevent weed seed from getting down into the soil. Leave the clippings behind as a natural mulch that will quickly break down and help with improving the soil beneath.

Aeration and de-thatching the lawn will also serve to promote grass to grow properly and will not encourage weeds unless the de-thatching is too aggressive, or the holes left by aeration are not filled in quickly.

Black medick (Medicago lupulina) *is one of a myriad of weeds that frequently pop up in turfgrass.*

Positively ID those weeds that are already there so that you know what you are dealing with and can decide which, if any, remedial action is most appropriate. For instance, are the weeds annual or perennial? If annual, they are easier to remove by digging or pulling them out by hand. If perennial, there is a good chance that they are rhizomatous, and thus more of a problem.

Manually removing weeds is often the most viable option. My favourite tool for the job is a very old, long, skinny knife that gets way down deep and slices off the roots. It takes a bunch of energy for perennial weeds to get back to the surface, just in time for them to be knocked back again until they are starved out. Annual weeds only need to be severed at the base and they will not regrow.

If the weeds are a broadleaf species, then an herbicide specific to broadleaf plants can be considered, which will not impact the grasses, though it will negatively impact the soil life. If the weeds are grasses, a broadleaf remedy will not be effective, and any herbicide applied to those weeds will also kill the grass. I emphasize, however, that applying herbicide is not advised unless extreme action is necessary as those chemicals will also negatively affect insects, not to mention children and pets. And unless the underlying conditions are changed, the weeds will return.

Assess the cultural practices being followed, such as whether the lawn is receiving enough moisture at the appropriate time. Or too much at the wrong times? Look to see if areas of the lawn are more compacted that others, or not at all. Is the lawn being mowed at the best height and with sharpened blades? Is it being fertilized properly so that it grows well, but not too lushly? Look at foot traffic areas, where grass is being trodden down. If people are not following pathways, then perhaps the pathways should be moved as people always take the best and shortest path to get where they are going. Then change those practices to promote the weed-free lawn that is desired.

Remediating a lawn does take time, so take photos of what it looked like at the beginning, so that you can see the progress being made.[6] —JM

My lawn is old and tired. How can I go about reviving it?

Let me count the ways.

1. Aerate it. You don't have to do this every year, unless your lawn is deeply compacted and the grass roots are shallow, extending only about 1 to 2 inches (2.5 to 5 centimetres) below the surface of the soil. Never aerate a lawn until it is at least one year old—truly, you can wait until it is at least five years old before aerating it for the first time. After you've aerated, you can sprinkle some grass seed into the holes left by the aerator and water them in. (This is one time you don't have to top-dress with a loam/compost mix before seeding.)

2. De-thatch it. The easiest way to do this is to manually rake it in the spring after the grass has started to green up. Don't tackle this task too early in the spring. If the ground is in the process of thawing and it is damp and cold, this is not the time to be out there with a rake. You'll do more harm than good to both your soil and your lawn. If you have a large lawn, you may wish to rent a power rake because de-thatching isn't fun and power rakes are.

3. Top-dress it with a thin (about 1 inch or 2.5 centimetres) layer of one part compost and two parts loam and seed it with a suitable turfgrass, such as sheep's fescue. Better yet, seed with a mixture of sheep's fescue and Dutch white clover (*Trifolium repens*).

4. A more extreme solution: remove the lawn entirely and plant a turfgrass alternative.

5. Another extreme solution: take up the existing lawn and resurface with fresh new sod. —SN

Grass will not grow where I want it to—under my conifer trees! Why not?

Successfully growing grass under a conifer, especially a spruce tree, is a matter of throwing time, energy, and resources into a deep well and watching them sink. It won't work!

The problem is that the environmental conditions for grass to grow well under a conifer tree just don't exist. Grass requires lots of sun. It also needs lots of water, nitrogen, and other nutrients. Conifer trees create lots of dense shade. That dense canopy means that rainfall seldom reaches the soil underneath. Conifers also require huge amounts of moisture. They have an extensive root system, with many of the roots just below the surface of the soil, and will be competing directly with the roots of the grasses. They leave little in the soil for grass to do well.

Another factor is that conifer needles drop all year long, often in great quantities, creating a great mulch for the tree that protects those shallow roots. Those needles also emit a gas that supresses germination of other species.[7] Additionally, the soil under these trees is usually compacted, partially due to those root systems. There just isn't a lot of soil for grass to root into. Look at the trees in any woodland or forest. Not much is growing directly underneath them for that reason.

Many people undertake remedial action for the environmental conditions by topping up the soil under the trees to provide a better base for the grass. They may also remove that lovely mulch, composting the needles, or sending them to the landfill. They also will spend a lot of time watering and fertilizing the newly sown seeds or lay down grass sod.

The net result is that the conifer tree says, "Thank you very much," and promptly takes up all the moisture and nutrients, leaving none for the grass. What is worse, though, is that by trying to establish grass under the tree, you may be affecting the health of the tree by disturbing and exposing its roots.

Much better is to remove the existing grass out to the drip line of the tree and allow the needles and cones to provide a natural mulch. Then both the tree and the remaining grass look intentional and well tended. A nice edging can add to the aesthetic and that whole area can also now be a fertile area for well-placed containers that love the shade and protection of the tree. That is what I have done, and I love it![8] —JM

Conifers have needs...very big needs. Grass doesn't stand a chance when it comes to competing with huge coniferous trees for nutrients, water, and sunlight.

Pond and
Aquatic Grasses

4

What is the difference between cattails and bulrushes?

Quite a lot actually! While the two names are used almost interchangeably, they are entirely different genera. Each has different root systems and other distinguishing features. One species is even called the cattail bulrush, just to make things even more confusing. You do not want to plant one thinking that it is the other or you may get quite the surprise, as cattails are highly aggressive whereas bulrushes are not so much.

The common cattail (*Typha latifolia*), a species in the grass family, can grow up to 6.5 to 9 feet tall (2 to 3 metres) under ideal conditions (we never get ideal conditions!). It has flower spikes on top of stiff stems, with linear leaves arranged down the stem. Both female and male flowers are on each spike and develop into the familiar, dark brown, fuzzy, cylindrical fruit. It grows in shallow water in anoxic (low oxygen) soils found in marshes, around ponds, and along riverbanks. It has rhizomatous roots that can spread aggressively. However, its primary means of reproduction are the multitude of fluffy seeds that float in the breeze to settle in the mud of the next likely place to grow.

Bulrushes, either hard-stem (*Schoenoplectus acutus*) or soft-stem (*S. tabernaemontani*), are reeds in the sedge family (Cyperaceae). At first glance they look similar to cattails; however, they are much less aggressive as they reproduce primarily through rhizomes rather than via seed and grow in deeper water. In fact, when both are present in a water body, the bulrushes will be in the water and the cattails along the margins. Oddly enough, should water dry up, bulrushes are much more drought tolerant than cattails.

Both have adapted to take oxygen from the air and transport it to their roots. They are both almost entirely edible and considered to be herbs.

Given the choice for your garden, choose bulrushes over cattails unless you have a very large area to fill, and only buy plants that have the full botanical name on the labels to be sure that you get what you want. It really is buyer beware in the case of bulrushes and cattails![1] —JM

Cattails, shown here, and bulrushes are highly attractive to birds and other wildlife.

How do I plant or transplant pond plants?

First off, all aquatic grasses should be planted with a clay-based topsoil that will hold its shape when wet. Avoid using any soil mix that has a lot of compost, manure, or peat as these materials are light and will literally float in the water. Not only that, but they can create issues with water quality. You can also use specialized potting mediums designed to promote stability of the pond system as well as encouraging good rooting of new plants.

Use plastic containers (with holes at the bottom) or open-mesh aquatic baskets, but ensure that the container is large enough for the mature plant. Aquatic grasses often grow at a faster rate than those on land and can quickly become root-bound. Pots can be weighted and placed on stands in the middle of the pond or along the sides on pond shelves.

Grasses can also be planted along the margins of the pond directly into the soil. Dig a hole as deep as the plant root ball and twice as wide. Position the plant in the hole, with the crown at the surface, and backfill with pond soil. A good idea is to place gravel on top of the soil to prevent erosion that could impact the pond system, especially the clarity of the water. To water, scoop out pond water and apply it to the plant to ensure that it gets acclimatized to its new ecosystem.

Monitor newly planted grasses to ensure they remain securely planted in their baskets or in the soil.[2]—JM

How do I fertilize pond grasses in containers or on pond shelves?

Depending on the quality of the pond water and whether it has nutrients in it, pond grasses may not need to be fertilized. This is especially the case if the pond contains fish, whose excrement provides a lot of nutrients in the form of nitrates. However, should you choose to fertilize your pond grasses, they are likely to be healthier, becoming larger and just generally happier.

But it is not just a matter of using liquid or granular fertilizers meant for soil. The results may be toxic to the plants there and may induce the proliferation of algae.

Instead, use pellets or spikes formulated for pond plants and ensure that they are inserted a number of inches into the pond soil or into the container holding the plant. The best time to fertilize is in the spring when the water is above 60°F (15°C), so that the nutrients can be readily absorbed by the grasses. But go easy, as the pond environment may be enough to provide many of the necessary nutrients. Evaluate the plants before you go ahead with a further round of fertilizer in any given season.[3]

Finally, what about your marginal plants that are planted into the ground? You won't need to fertilize them, as the plants will take up some nutrients from the pond itself, which should be sufficient. If your marginal plants are in containers, however, you may need to add fertilizer to promote showy blooms. Use slow-release fertilizer tablets specifically formulated for pond plants in containers.[4] —JM & SN

Do I need to remove my pond plants before winter? How do I safely keep them indoors?

You'll need to know the hardiness of your plants to determine whether they can withstand winter. Hardy marginal grasses and other hardy plants can stay put where they are. Cut back the foliage of hardy marginal plants before the snow flies so that excess plant debris doesn't fall into the pond and potentially cause issues with algae once spring arrives and the water warms up.

If you're a bit nervous about losing your hardy pond plants, you can trim them, then submerge their baskets in the water so that they can take advantage of the slightly warmer water temperatures at the bottom of the pond.

Plants that are not hardy will need to be brought indoors for the winter. Lift them out of the pond (including the baskets they are growing in) and place them in large plastic totes filled with water. The plants will need sunlight and warmth (but not too much heat). If you have only a few tropical pond plants, you can place them individually in pots filled with water and grow them as you would houseplants.[5] —SN

It can be a bit of work to prepare your pond plants for the winter, but taking the time to do so will minimize your losses to the cold.

How do I create a container pond or one for my tabletop? Which plant selections are good for such a project?

Container ponds or pots are great for those with a smaller space or who prefer not to undertake the work and expense, not to mention finding the space in the garden, for a full pond.

These smaller garden features serve many purposes, including moderating low humidity levels near the container and providing water for wildlife, and even habitat in a few instances. They are also wonderful for gardeners to sit beside, and, if a bubbler or mini-fountain is included, the sound of the water can be therapy all by itself.

It may seem complicated or hard to create and maintain a container pond. But it's not really.

First, select your location. It should receive four to six hours of direct sunlight a day. You do not want it to be in full sun for more than that to deter the growth of algae. Plus, the small amount of water in the vessel will get overly warm for plant roots and any wildlife living in the container. Should your container be stepped down or sloped, so that there is a section with shallower water, place the container where it will get more shade, as shallower water will heat even faster. Patios, decks, balconies, and the garden itself are all options for placement of the containers. They can be tucked away or be a central focal point. The choice is yours, but before you fill it with water, be sure that the container is where it should be. Water is heavy, roughly 8 pounds (3.6 kilograms) per gallon (4.5 litres), and you do not want to be lugging that around willy-nilly!

Next, the container. Literally any style, material, and size of container can be used. It should be watertight (of course) and a size that suits the location. Glazed ceramic pots are ideal, especially if they do not have a drainage hole. If they do, seal up the hole with silicone caulking, and allow it to dry for a least a day, preferably two. You can also use a clay pot, so long as you apply at least two coats of sealant. Wood, especially those oak barrels cut in half, and many metal containers are excellent but need to have a pond liner at least ½ inch (1.2 centimetres) thick placed inside.

Container ponds are fun projects that can bring a water feature to your balcony or deck. These tubs are a good start to designing a rustic-style container pond.

Then decide whether to use still or aerated water. A small pump or bubbler is excellent at reducing the growth of algae and preventing mosquitoes from laying eggs. It also prevents stagnation. A bubbler or mini-fountain can be purchased or fabricated and can be electrical or solar powered. Make sure to weigh it down with stones or bricks so that it is stable and not moving around. If opting for still water, do use a mosquito dunk, which is a compressed cake of *Bacillus thuringiensis* var. *israelensis* (Bti).[6] It is a natural insecticide that will not affect wildlife or plants.

Arrange perching bricks or stones for the plants you wish to place inside the container, then have fun playing with the design you are envisioning. A few grasses placed to great effect are more striking than many crowded in, and it is oh-so-tempting to buy more than you need. You can integrate grasses with other aquatic plants, from those loving being fully immersed in water to the more marginal plants, depending on the size of your container. Suitable grasses include dwarf cattail (*Typha minima*) and dwarf papyrus (*Cyperus haspan*) as well as horsetails (*Equisetum* spp.) and sweet flags (*Acorus* spp.). Both rushes and sedges are also ideal for pond containers.

Now it is time to fill the container. Rainwater is best but tap water can be used. Let it sit at least a day and preferably two so the chlorine can dissipate.

Once your pond container is up and running, all that is needed is to keep it topped up with water periodically and enjoy it![7] —JM

Are there any pond plants I should avoid growing?

This is something you definitely want to look into before you go shopping for pond plants (or any plants!). You never want to risk having an invasive species overrun your pond, pose a threat to other species of plants or animals, or possibly spread to other areas. Businesses that sell plants are supposed to be regulation-savvy and should not ever offer invasive plants to consumers, but sometimes the knowledge base is not present, particularly when plants are grown in one province and shipped to another. Weed acts vary from province to province; what is invasive in one area may not be in another.

Flowering rush (*Butomus umbellatus*) is an example of an invasive species that was introduced to North America from Africa, Asia, and Europe, likely due to its strikingly beautiful flowers. Unfortunately, we now know that flowering rush can outcompete native pond plants. In a one-two punch, it spreads by seed as well as via the bulbils it grows from its rhizomatous roots. It can grow along the margins of wetlands as well as in the water itself, and its aggressive spread negatively impacts water quality and affects the habitat of fish and other aquatic life. In recreational waterways, its root systems can prevent swimmers and boaters from enjoying their activities. This plant is occasionally still found in online and mail-order catalogues, so be on the lookout for it and do not purchase it.

Reed canary grass (*Phalaris arundinacea*) is actually a grass native to many parts of Canada, and we don't normally pick native plants for the invasive list, but, as you'll see, reed canary grass is certainly a good candidate. It is a marginal plant that aggressively spreads via rhizomes, choking out other vegetation. It takes up huge amounts of water in its bid to take over the world, seriously affecting other plants growing nearby. When plants like this outcompete everything around them, biodiversity is reduced.

The key to ensuring that your ponds are free of invasive plants is to not accidentally bring them in from another place. Be careful to purchase plants from reputable sources. Do your research so you know what types of plants should not be grown in your area.[8] —SN

It is possible that in the late nineteenth century, ships moving across waterways helped transport flowering rush plants when ballast water was dumped. This invasive species should not be cultivated.

Grasses You Can Eat

5

What edible grasses can we grow on the prairies?

It is interesting. A great number of herbivorous grazing mammals are able to eat grass with impunity, gaining all the nutrients they need. Whereas we humans cannot. This is because those herbivorous grazing mammals have evolved digestive systems that break down the cellulose found in grass foliage. Although humans can eat grass leaves, it just isn't the best source of nutrients for us and can cause some stomach aches along the way. However, humans have found other ways to use grasses for food — typically from the seeds, either whole or ground into flour. Sometimes we can eat the roots, too. Often grass foliage is juiced to extract the goodness from the leaves, with the cellulose fibre discarded or sufficiently broken down to be digestible. In many cultures, edible grasses are used for medicinal purposes as well.

Wheat, barley, rye, oats, millet, corn, and rice are known as major cereal crops. The grains from these grasses provide calories and nutrients for our diets. However, there are several other grasses that are perfectly edible and tasty.

Crabgrass (*Digitaria sanguinalis*) these days is grown as a forage grass, yet it is very nutritious and has been used medicinally in the past.

Orchardgrass (*Dactylis glomerata*) is another pasture grass that is edible, but there are better things to eat as it won't supply enough nutrients for us humans. It's not worth bothering with unless you are very hungry.

Goosegrass (*Galium aparine*), on the other hand, can be used as a cooked green when it is picked in the spring when it is young.

Wheatgrass (*Triticum* spp.) is the young blades of newly sprouted seeds and is used to make juice for smoothies. It is a good source of nutrients, and, as a bonus, it is gluten-free.

Wild rice's (*Zizania* spp.) grains are a culinary delight.

Sorghum (*Sorghum bicolor*) is native to Africa but is found in the wild around the world these days, and the small grains can be harvested and ground into flour.

Wild rice is a native North American grass.

Foxtail grasses (*Setaria* spp.) can be harvested for their grains, which are similar to wild rice.

Wild oats (*Avena* spp.) and Canada wild rye (*Elymus canadensis*) are often considered weeds, yet both were harvested by Indigenous peoples for their grain.

There are a multitude of other grasses that are used for their juices and seeds, including timothy (*Phleum pratense*), which sometimes is called cattails (just to confuse us even more); brome (*Bromus* spp.); bluegrass (*Poa* spp.); and switchgrass (*Panicum* spp.).

Finally, we must not forget lemongrass (*Cymbopogon citratus*). While it is not hardy for the prairies, it is available as an annual herb, with the foliage used to flavour soups, teas, and other dishes.[1] —JM

Can I grow wheat, oats, rye, and millet in my garden?

Yes, you can! Your yields will be higher if you are able to grow many plants, of course. But if you just want to produce some grains to mill into flour for a few loaves of bread, you can do it in a much smaller garden space.

There are several different types of millet, including the extremely showy ornamental pearl or cattail types (*Pennisetum glaucum*) such as 'Purple Majesty'. (Look for that one to put into containers—it's a standout!) Proso millet (*Panicum miliaceum*) and foxtail millet (*Setaria italica*) are commonly grown as food and forage crops. Millet really loves long, hot summers. Depending on the variety, the days to maturity range from sixty to ninety. Millet likes fertile soil, so amend your soil with compost before sowing and add a side dressing of approximately ½ inch (1.2 centimetres) of compost midway through the growing season.

As we've mentioned on page 49, fall rye is commonly used as a cover crop to help build soil. You can also grow rye to harvest its seeds. Plant fall rye during the autumn (usually in September) the previous year before you want to harvest it. The plants can take between 120 and 150 days to mature. You can choose to grow spring rye instead, in which case you'll sow in May.

Oats are another crop we can grow in our gardens so long as we offer proper irrigation (they don't tolerate drought). When you source oat seeds for your garden, choose hull-less types so you don't have as much work to do when processing the grain after harvest. Oats take a minimum of 45 days to maturity.

We discuss growing wheatgrass (*Triticum* spp.) on page 84 of this book, but you can also grow it to harvest its seeds for grain. You can choose to plant spring wheat, which is sown as soon as the soil is warm enough to work in the spring, or winter wheat, which is sown in the fall and harvested the following year. Wheat prefers nutrient-rich soil and benefits from amendments of compost. You'll also need to keep up with watering, especially in the heat.

One thing to note when growing these grasses in your garden: the seeds are absolute magnets for many species of birds and they will pluck out every one they can find in your garden bed right after you've sown them. They will also come around when it's harvest time and give you a run for your money. To combat this, cover your seed bed with row cover fabric until the plants have germinated. To protect your fall harvest, you can set up a tent using stakes and bird-friendly (very fine mesh) netting. Leave a few plants uncovered to treat the birds, though—they deserve it![2] —SN

Ornamental millet varieties are absolute standouts in containers.

How do I grow wheatgrass?

If you're big on juicing, wheatgrass (*Triticum* spp.) is probably one of your go-tos. It can be a bit pricey to purchase fully grown-out trays of it in the supermarket, but if you can find a bulk supplier for seeds, you can grow your own and save a considerable amount of dough.

Most people growing wheatgrass for juicing prefer to use hard red winter seeds as they have a wider leaf blade than spring wheat—important when that's the part you're extracting juice from! You can certainly use spring wheat seeds if that's all you can get.

You can grow wheatgrass in sprouting trays that have been purchased at the garden centre or repurpose a food-safe container from a takeout meal. Ensure the tray has drainage holes in the base and set it into a saucer. The tray doesn't need to be very deep as you'll need to put only about 1 inch (2.5 centimetres) of growing medium in it. I usually grow wheatgrass in a commercial potting mix, but I have also had great success growing it on fibre mats such as hemp or coir. If you choose to use a soil-based medium, don't collect soil out of your garden beds for this project. Avoid using soil that has polymer crystals in it. You won't need any slow-release fertilizer as your plants won't be growing for very long.

To help speed up germination, soak your seeds in water for twelve hours before sowing them into your trays. Put your seeds in a jar and cover them with at least twice the amount of water as seeds. Before planting, drain and rinse the seeds. Then you're ready to plant! Moisten the soil in your trays before you get started. Wheatgrass seeds are sown intensively, close together. Don't worry too much about spacing, just ensure they aren't piled on top of each other. Gently press them into the growing medium so that they are just covered. Wheatgrass takes two to three days to germinate. Set the tray in a space that has bright but indirect light. Keep up with watering. As the tray is shallow, you may need to water more than once per day once the plants begin to grow (but be careful not to overwater).

Wheatgrass is usually ready to harvest ten to twelve days after germination. Something important to note if you are juicing your harvested wheatgrass: those leaves are seriously hard on your average juicer and can wreck it after only a few uses. Spend the extra money to get a juicer that is meant for working with wheatgrass.—SN

Be sure to plant wheatgrass in succession for a continuous supply for juicing. Photo courtesy of Rob Normandeau.

Can you give some tips for growing cat grass?

Orchardgrass (*Dactylis glomerata*), wheatgrass, alfalfa (*Medicago sativa*), barley (*Hordeum* spp.), oats (*Avena* spp.), and rye (*Elymus canadensis*) are all part of a category of different types of grasses generically named cat grass. These grasses are grown for consumption by our pet cats (and some dog owners offer it to their beloved canines, too). Cats are predominantly carnivores, but there is some research suggesting that the fibre in grass can help with their digestion. Grass can also be a source of folic acid, which they may not get in their kibble, if it hasn't been fortified with it. If your cat lives indoors, she doesn't have access to turfgrass (and if you use herbicides on your lawn, you're not going to want your outdoor cat munching on it). Growing some grass in a tray indoors solves that issue. Some cats—like mine—enjoy pulling it up by its roots out of the tray I grow it in, gnawing on part of it like chewing gum, then abandoning what's left of the tiny plant on the floor for me to clean up. She may be careless with it when it comes to chowing down, but while the seeds are waiting to sprout in the tray, she inspects it daily to see what stage everything is at and is sorely disappointed when it isn't ready. As with wheatgrass, it's useful to have multiple trays of cat grass growing at once so that you never run out and face a displeased feline. There is no special trick to growing cat grass—sow it and care for it just as you would the wheatgrass you enjoy. Your cat will take care of the harvesting.[3]—SN

Smudge eyeballs the cat grass to determine if it's ready for consumption.

Are chia, quinoa, buckwheat, and amaranth grasses?

We might be forgiven for thinking that this quartet of grain-producing plants are grasses, given that it is grasses that produce the seeds that we call grains and cereals that are the primary carbohydrate supply across the world for humans, livestock, and wildlife.

In fact, these grain-producing plants are pseudocereals, being dicot species grown for their seeds or fruit that are used as cereals. They are known to have high levels of proteins and fibre and are gluten-free.

Amaranth (*Amaranthus* spp.) is a genus of the Amaranthaceae family, grown for their seeds and as ornamental plants. Chia (*Salvia hispanica*) belongs to the mint family, Lamiaceae. Buckwheat (*Fagopyrum esculentum*) is part of the same family as rhubarb, that being Polygonaceae. Quinoa (*Chenopodium quinoa*) belongs to the same genus, *Chenopodium*, as spinach, chard, and beets and is related to amaranth, being part of the same botanical family.

Pseudocereals are nutrient dense, delicious, and increasingly part of a healthy diet. What they aren't are species of the grass family, Poaceae.[4]—JM

Amaranth is a prolific seed producer. The ornamental types are vibrantly coloured and showy.

Is corn a grass? How do I grow it successfully on the prairies?

It doesn't quite look like the other grasses we know, but yes, corn (*Zea mays*) is certainly a grass! Although we can grow many varieties of popcorn, ornamental corn (sometimes called flint corn), and field corn (also called dent or cow corn) on the prairies, I am going to focus primarily on sweet corn here, as it's the one we commonly put on our dinner plates. Corn is an annual grass that was first domesticated in Mexico approximately 8,700 years ago. It is thought to be derived from the wild corn (*Balsas teosinte*).

Corn is a warm-season crop and generally needs a long season to produce harvestable cobs. Corn seeds typically won't germinate if the soil and ambient temperature are less than 50°F (10°C), and the ideal temperature range for growing corn is 60 to 75°F (15 to 24°C). You may have heard of the term Corn Heat Units (CHUs). This is a temperature index used by corn producers to determine if the climate in a certain region is warm enough to allow corn varieties to fully mature there. Most sweet corn varieties need 2,200 CHUs to mature. Some seed catalogues will publish this information so you can match up the days to maturity and the CHUs of a specific variety with the average temperatures in your area and figure out if it's worth slapping down a few dollars for those particular seeds.

We talked about identifying varieties of sweet corn using kernel sweetness on pages 86–87 of *The Prairie Gardener's Go-To for Vegetables*, so I'm not going to go into that here, but depending on the type of sweet corn you are growing, you will have to isolate it from other types to prevent cross-pollination. There are a couple of easy ways to accomplish this. If you are planting more than one variety of corn, ensure there is at least 250 to 700 feet (76 to 213 metres) of space separating the varieties. Another option is to stagger your plantings of different varieties by at least two weeks. If you do this, also make sure the varieties you plant have different days to maturity. You don't want to stagger your planting time and then realize that the varieties are flowering at the same time.

Corn needs well-drained soil and plenty of water to grow and produce delicious, sweet kernels. Be sure you can provide the right conditions and select the best varieties for your garden for success![5] —SN

Looks like successful pollination occurred here!

Pests, Pathogens, and Other Problems

6

In our book *The Prairie Gardener's Go-To for Pests and Diseases*, we covered common problematic plant enemies of ornamental and turfgrasses, such as slugs, aphids, and powdery mildew. We're narrowing our focus for this book to give some tips about how to deal with issues that are specific to turfgrasses, including snow mould, fairy ring, chinch bugs, and dew worms. We'll also cover some of the problems that can plague ornamental grasses, such as rust and anthracnose.

As always, we recommend practising Integrated Pest Management when it comes to dealing with anything troubling your grasses and other plants. Watch for any changes in their health, signs that something may not be right, or physical evidence that there is a pest or pathogen at work. If the problem is merely cosmetic, or if it doesn't have wide-ranging or long-lasting effects that can seriously harm the plants, there is no need to take action. If something needs to be done, however, we're here to give you tips on how to proceed using methods that are the least harmful to the environment. We'll also offer some preventive strategies to work on for the future, so that your grasses are as healthy and stress-free as possible. —SN & JM

My ornamental grasses are showing signs of wilting and yellowing. Should I be concerned?

When grasses are signalling that they are suffering by wilting, yellowing, or just generally looking unhealthy, there can be a number of factors at play, either separately or in combination.

Start with the weather. Has it been too cold for the grass in question? Warm-season grasses are not thrilled with unseasonable cold. Those cool-season grasses are just fine, so if you can compare how a number of grasses are doing, you can likely determine if our wonky weather is the culprit. But perhaps it has been stinking hot. In that case, just about all plants are going to be wilting in the heat. If they bounce back after the temperature has dropped, then that is the problem. Wildfire smoke, damage from hail, and excessive winds can also be primary or secondary causes for symptoms of distress.

Next, look where the grasses are sited. Are they getting too much direct sunlight? Or not enough? A grass meant to be in dappled shade is going to hate being fried all day long and vice versa. If the light is good, then look at the soil. Is it compacted, with poor drainage? Or too rich with organic matter, given most grasses prefer soil on the lean side?

Assuming the grasses are planted where they should be, then look at cultural practices. Are they getting enough water? Or not enough? Many grasses are drought tolerant, but there is a limit, and once soil is past the permanent wilting point, then grasses will for sure wilt to the point of death. Other species need moister soil. If they are being overwatered, they will turn yellow, especially if the too-soggy soil means their roots are rotting. Are they being fertilized too much, promoting overly lush growth that keels over? Too much fertilizer can create toxic conditions, which will lead to yellowing. Are they too crowded and do they not have enough access to necessary resources? Then it may be time to divide them.

A natural cause of yellowing could be natural dieback as the plants age out and are at the end of their life cycle. They could even be meant to turn yellow (or other colours) as the season progresses. It seems silly, but sometimes, depending on conditions, plants will turn different colours than advertised, and yellow is often the colour of choice.

Finally, look at the potential for pests and diseases. Generally, grasses have little to worry about from insects or pathogens, but there are a few that target grasses. Rust, anthracnose, leaf spots, and mildews could be an issue. Alternatively, insects such as mites and aphids could be present. Or there could be nematodes, slugs, or soil-dwelling insects eating the roots. There could even be critter damage, varying from deer to rabbits to rodents chomping away.

All of which is to say that diagnosing the issue means thinking of all the possibilities, checking for signs and symptoms, and monitoring for improvement once you decide on a course of action but being ready to look for alternatives if the plants are not responding.

We all wish that plants could talk so they could tell us what is wrong. But failing that, we all need to be good plant issue diagnosticians![1] —JM

My turfgrass has gross web-like patches all over it after the snow melts. What is this and what should I do about it?

There are several types of fungi that cause snow mould. Small dark patches of pink snow mould (*Microdochium nivale*) may appear in the spring after a long slow melt, while the mycelia of Coprinus (cottony) snow mould (*Coprinus psychromorbidus*) resembles tufts of cotton balls. Gardeners are probably most familiar with grey snow mould (also known as Typhula blight, caused by *Typhula* spp.), which will cause turfgrass to mat in brown or grey clumps. Snow moulds often occur annually, in the same location, and the spores may be spread by foot traffic and mowers. While there isn't much you can do to control the speed and timing of the spring snowmelt (or the wet autumns that may also be contributors to snow mould growth), to reduce the occurrence of this issue, watch your watering in the autumn and do not offer the lawn too much water going into dormancy. Do not use high-nitrogen fertilizers too late in the season. Keep the grass mowed (but not too short) until just before freeze-up and remove or shred fallen leaves and other plant debris. When you notice the snow piles in your yard beginning to diminish in the spring, shave large piles down and shovel the snow evenly onto the lawn to help it melt faster. Once the lawn dries, the mould will disappear, and you can rake the lawn (but be sure to disinfect the garden tools afterward). Later in the spring, remove excess thatch, if necessary.[2] —SN

Snow mould can be a regular and very annoying occurrence, but there are measures you can take to mitigate it.

How do I deal with fairy ring?

Fairy ring is caused by basidiomycete fungi. Although you won't realize your soil contains the fungi until the telltale "rings" of darker green grass and small mushrooms appear, the actuality is that the fungi have probably been working deep underground for a very long time, feeding on dead organic matter. The fungi thrive in dry areas with low soil fertility. Fungicides will not remove fairy ring, and pulling out the mushrooms will not get rid of it. Instead, it is necessary to de-stress and rejuvenate the lawn to combat the fungi. Bear in mind that this process can take several years. You can see why control of fairy ring is so difficult!

Improve water filtration by using a garden fork to make small holes across the area affected by the ring. Push the fork into the soil to a depth of at least ten inches (twenty-five centimetres) for best results. Water the area deeply and frequently (but be sure to adjust for rainfall amounts). If the ring is small, you may be able to lift out the entire affected area by digging. Dispose of the pieces of sod in the garbage and do not compost them. Do not allow them to touch the bare soil or they will spread the fungi. Although fairy ring is usually viewed as a huge annoyance, it's actually a sign of nature at work, responding to the conditions of the soil.[3] — SN

Fairy ring is one of the most common complaints we hear from homeowners. They are extremely persistent but you can eventually deter them by heaping loads of TLC *on your lawn.*

My ornamental grasses have tiny orange-red blisters on them. What is going on?

Chances are your grasses have been infected by a rust fungus. There are around 8,000 species of rust, all belonging to the order Pucciniales, and many are very host specific. Some of the rust fungus species require two hosts (heteroecious); others only a single host (autoecious). Unfortunately, many rusts have hosts that are grasses, including agricultural cereal crops and especially stem rust of wheat (*Puccinia graminis* f. sp. *tritici*). Not just the grasses in our gardens!

Rust fungi are obligate parasites, meaning they only live on live plants, and they get all they need to live on from the host. They create a structure called a haustorium, part plant cell wall and part fungus cell wall, which is the means for the fungi to obtain nutrients from their host.[4] What those structures look like to us are rusty, orange, or brown lesions or spots on the leaves and stems of our grasses. Often, they appear as dots or speckles to begin with and may develop into bumps, and are most apparent on the undersides of the leaves. Sometimes you can spot the structures developing fruiting bodies, where spores will be released to go to other likely hosts.

In most instances, the infection grows from the ground up, so if you spot a problem close to the ground you have a good chance of getting a handle on it. But act fast!

Wet foliage, when temperatures hover between 68 and 86°F (20 to 30°C), is prime conditions for the fungus to infect your grasses, especially when foliage stays wet for more than six hours. It is hard to do anything about rainfall leaving foliage wet for hours, but there are steps to take to lessen the chances, such as providing the best airflow you can for your grasses. Avoid overcrowding them or placing them where they are too sheltered. When watering, do so in the morning to avoid the foliage being still wet by nightfall, and water the base of the plants, not the foliage.

As soon as you spot any infection, remove the leaves and place them in the garbage. Ensure any plant debris on the ground is cleared away. Add some compost around the plant as some TLC, as any grass infected by rust will be weakened and more prone to other infections or insects a-coming. You can apply a foliar spray that contains sulphur, which changes the pH on the foliage to more of an acidic base, acting to prevent the fungus from invading the cell walls. If you experienced rust in a previous year and the conditions are ripe for another outbreak, you can proactively spray your grasses with a baking soda and water mixture, a Bordeaux mixture (copper sulphate, lime, and water), or even two Aspirins dissolved in a quart (two litres) of water.[5] You can take another two Aspirins for yourself, too, for the headache you get from the frustration of dealing with this pathogen! —JM

Careful application of supplemental irrigation can help prevent the spread of rust diseases in ornamental grasses.

There are some dark lesions on the stems and leaves of my grasses. What causes this?

Anthracnose is caused by the fungus *Colletotrichum gloeosporioides* and can affect cool-season and warm-season ornamental and turf grasses. Affected plants may exhibit dark spots on the leaves and stems (depending on the species of grass, those spots can be more yellow in colour or even pinkish red). Turfgrass may die out in spots and become patchy. The fungal setae may appear, looking like black threads on the blades of grass. Ornamental grasses may turn brown in sections.

A long, dry, hot summer is desirable to prevent anthracnose. The fungus prefers to proliferate in damp conditions.

If you notice signs of anthracnose on your grasses, do everything you can to keep it from spreading. If it is in your ornamental grasses, trim off any dead or infected stems and dispose of them in the garbage, not the compost. Clean your tools with rubbing alcohol. Clean up any plant debris lying on the ground beneath the plant. If your grasses are sun lovers, ensure they are sited properly—don't stuff them into a dark, wet location where they are stressed and more susceptible to infections by pathogens. Hold back the fertilizer as too much nitrogen will cause lush growth that is irresistible to fungi.

If you think your turfgrass has anthracnose, it may help to raise the blade height on your mower. This causes less stress to grass. Do not water in the evening. Aerating the lawn can help as well.[6]—SN

Ants are invading my lawn. What can I do?

We sure love to hate ants. Yet ants are beneficial, indeed necessary, for a healthy environment. Collectively, they contribute hugely as pollinators for plants, aerators of soils, seed dispersal agents, and decomposers, munching their way through plant detritus. They also eat the larvae of certain lawn pests. Yet we view them as pests. They bug us by climbing on our legs and getting into things, most especially when they bite us because we are bugging them!

We seek to kill them when they are in our lawns for just being themselves and causing cosmetic damage. It is a frustrating exercise as there are billions more ants than us, and they will just come right back, assuming the conditions are what they prefer. What is really desirable is that their populations be in balance, so that there are enough of them to do their jobs but not so many that they are out of control.

What ants really love are dry, fine soils with a low organic and moisture content. They want dry, safe houses, just like us. Many times, that is exactly what is provided, as lawns are rarely disturbed to improve the underlying soil. So, the goal should be to amend that soil to be less desirable for the ants. Just like us, they will then pick up and move somewhere else better for them.

Improving the soil is a matter of raking in compost at the beginning of the season and at the end. The compost will sift down into the root zone and over time will enhance the soil's capacity for moisture, along with boosting the organic matter content. Deep water occasionally so that the moisture gets right down into the subsoil, avoiding frequent shallow watering that doesn't penetrate deeply, and you will be well on the way to moving those ants along.

Keeping the grass slightly higher will also keep moisture in longer. Should you care to go further, sowing in different grasses and other ground-hugging species with differing root zones will assist the work in progress, especially if the species sown encourages wildlife to come feed on seeds, worms, and, yes, ants.

Short-term measures to knock back populations can include raking flat any nests. The ants will be mad, so wear rubber boots! You can also do some spot work, by pouring boiling water onto nests. It will kill the grass as well as disrupting populations temporarily.

An effective measure that will draw some chuckles from the neighbours is to fill a pot (with holes at the bottom) with soil and a sugary cereal and place it over the ant nest. The ants will climb up into the pot, drawn by the sugar; then you just take the pot, soil, and ants to a place where it doesn't matter that they will set up a new home.

Avoid using home remedies or commercial applications meant to kill ants. These products may kill of some of them, but they are certain to badly affect other soil life and insects dwelling in the grass as well as being a danger to pets and people.[7] —JM

Is there anything that can be done about chinch bugs in my lawn?

In one of the first classes I took when studying horticulture, our instructor told us that insect identification was pretty daunting. True—but not exactly encouraging! Fortunately, one way to narrow things down a bit is to examine the mouthparts of the species in question. Most insects have either chewing or piercing-sucking mouthparts. Chinch bugs (*Blissus leucopterus*) take all that one step beyond: they have sucking mouthparts that drain the juices out of turfgrass, and, just to be ornery, they also inject a toxic saliva that prevent plants from taking up water. Affected grass will turn brown and then die.

You'd be hard pressed to see chinch bugs at work—try to spot tiny black adults with white wings, especially at the end of July or late August—but you will smell them after you've mowed the lawn, as their crushed bodies give off a foul odour. Chinch bugs breed prolifically and can produce up to four generations every year, which, from a gardener's perspective, isn't very polite at all.

Prevent the insects from overwintering in your lawn by removing heavy thatch in the fall and raking up leaf litter. An overly lush lawn is appealing to chinch bugs, so minimize use of high-nitrogen fertilizer to keep them at bay. Make sure you keep up with a regular, consistent watering schedule, especially in hot and dry weather, which chinch bugs love.[8]—SN

Chinch bugs are hugely motivated by dry, hot conditions, and they will do massive amounts of damage to your lawn in a very short period of time.

Dew worms are making lumpy mounds in my lawn. What can I do about them?

Dew worms (*Lumbricus terrestris*) are a large (up to eleven inches or thirty centimetres long) earthworm native to Europe but now found across North America. They are also known as night crawlers. You don't often see these worms, as they burrow in deep tunnels beneath the surface of the soil, but you'll see can't-miss evidence of their activity as lumps and bumps on your lawn, especially after a rain or if you've irrigated heavily. These mounds look like they are made of sand, but they are actually the castings (excreta) of the worms as they move around under your turfgrass, feed, and periodically surface to deposit their waste.

There are a few ways to deal with the mess dew worms make (although bear in mind there is no real way to prevent their litter completely as it's a natural process and the worms will just keep working overtime).

1. Moisture will increase worm activity levels, so it may be possible to limit their presence by watering less. The downside, of course, is a less lush lawn.
2. Sprinkling gypsum (calcium sulphate) over the casting mounds will cause them to dry up. You can then rake them smooth.
3. Rent a lawn roller and try to manually work out the bumps. You may have to do this every year.
4. Dress the lawn with a soil mix of equal parts compost, topsoil, and peat or coir, rake it out to level it, and overseed with grass seed.
5. Aerate the lawn annually.

As annoying as they are, dew worms are food for many species of wildlife, including birds such as robins. Certain types of beetles, as well as centipedes, also prey on dew worms. Hopefully knowing that makes you feel better when confronted with the hillocks of castings on your lawn.[9]—SN

These telltale mounds containing a centre tunnel are the signature of dew worms.

I'm having trouble with Richardson's ground squirrels on my lawn. They are also digging up my ornamental grasses. What can I do to deter them?

The Richardson's ground squirrel (*Urocitellus richardsonii*) is seldom given its full name, which was bestowed on it in honour of the naturalist John Richardson, who first collected specimens of them back in 1820. Instead, they are called gophers or prairie gophers, along with their close relation, the black-tailed prairie dog (*Cynomys ludovicianus*). Which is wrong for both species. They are squirrels, not gophers, and belong to a totally different family (Geomyidae), with the northern pocket gopher (*Thomomys talpoides*) being the gopher we see most often. It drives naturalists wild to hear all these species lumped together!

Gardeners are driven wild too, but for different reasons.

All these "gophers" are ground dwellers, creating extensive tunnels underneath our feet. The exits can be a trap for the unwary. You can tell if you have a ground squirrel, prairie dog, or pocket gopher by the type of hole you find. If it is neat and tidy, about five inches (thirteen centimetres) in diameter, it is a ground squirrel or prairie dog. If the exit comes out at a slant with a mound of soil before it, then it is a pocket gopher.

We would all prefer that they weren't in our lawns or munching on our other grasses. But we have created the problems they cause us, because we have been busy ruining their natural habitat. So, they move to where there is less construction and agricultural activity and where there is lots of lovely food and fewer predators. So, they are labelled as a pest, and are shot, poisoned, and displaced indiscriminately. However, they are an important species for the prairie ecosystem, being food for coyotes and raptors for the four months of the year they are above ground.

So, what to do?

Poison has long been the go-to course of control. There is considerable debate about poison, however, as poisoned squirrels are then consumed by predators further up the food chain to their detriment. Plus, soil can be contaminated if the squirrels decompose in their burrows. Due to the environmental knock-on effects, these poisons are being increasingly restricted. Not only that, but the squirrels quickly come back.

Biological controls are a more sustainable way to go. Ground squirrels prefer open meadows for their habitat. Changing up your garden to include a variety of middling to taller plants, including grasses, along with trees and shrubs, will go a long way to discouraging them. If they do not have that open view, they cannot see potential predators and will deem it an unsafe location. Encouraging biodiversity within the garden will also encourage potential predators including ferruginous hawks to drop by for a snack. The combination of uneven lines of sight and potential predators is dynamite for moving them along, especially if you build perching spots for the birds to land on while they scan the garden. A few decoys are a great help too, either static or motion activated, especially if they are fitted with sounds.

Live-trapping and releasing far away is another option. There are a few other deterrents, such as packing soggy, stinky coffee grounds into the holes. These critters hate the smell and feel of those grounds. Some say it doesn't work, but in my experience, it does to a degree, plus you are introducing a natural material that faintly acidifies the soil and improves soil texture! Also, a solution made from three tablespoons castor oil, one tablespoon liquid dish soap, and one gallon (four litres) of water may have an effect when sprayed into their burrows. Consider whether you are leaving ready food sources available, such as garbage, open compost piles, and feeding stations for birds. If the problem is severe, you may need to rethink how you manage those items.

Finally, if they are driving you thoroughly bonkers, call in the professionals who will know an effective and humane way to lose at least this year's population from your garden.[10] —JM

Richardson's ground squirrels are absolutely adorable, but oh, what pests!

What are those tracks and tunnels in my lawn this spring? What made them?

This is the work of voles, a common rodent pest on the prairies. There are several species that live in this part of Canada, but meadow voles (*Microtus pennsylvanicus*) and prairie voles (*M. ochrogaster*) are usually the culprits. When you first see a vole, it's easy to mistake it for a mouse, but voles are a bit stockier and have rounder snouts and short, fur-covered tails. (Mice generally have long, naked tails.) Voles are not welcome in the garden at any time of year. In the summer, they'll snack on pretty much any vegetable. If your summer squash or pea pods are suddenly sporting tiny, neat rows of teeth marks, you'll know who to blame.

In the winter and early spring, voles are at their most annoying and destructive phase. They tunnel just below the soil surface and hide beneath the security of a blanket of snow to feed on perennial plant roots and gnaw on tree trunks. In some cases, they do enough harm to actually girdle trees. They damage lawns with their tracks and tunnels.

Fortunately, there are several preventive measures you can take to discourage these tiny destroyers. Here are a few to try.

1. Cut your lawn short in late autumn. This forces voles out of their hiding spots in the tall grass. Ensure you collect the grass clippings after you mow or they'll use them for cover.

2. Remove all plant debris such as dead leaves, fallen branches, and dead fruit. A clean garden will make voles think twice about where they want to reside for the winter.

3. If you don't use your compost bins in the winter, seal them shut or voles (and mice) will use them as five-star hotels.

4. Protect your immature trees by using plastic or wire mesh tree guards. Sink the guards six inches (fifteen centimetres) below the soil line. Consider where your average snow line is and ensure your guards surpass that height. (Voles can climb snowbanks, and they will if they see a nice juicy exposed part of a tree trunk.)

If you're faced with this ghastly sight when the snow melts in the spring, you'll know that voles have been very busy.

5. If you're okay with killing voles, you can bait some snap-type mouse traps with peanut butter in the autumn and try to catch as many as you can before the snow flies. Vole populations can be very high at that time of year, however, so keeping up is a challenge. As well, I don't recommend traps when you have pets or young children in the garden.

6. You don't have to deal with voles alone. You can always hire a pest control company to help keep them in check.[11] —**SN**

What grasses are weeds? How do I control them?

There is no sugar-coating it. There are a number of grasses that are outright weeds; that is, in the sense that they are prolific in their growth to the detriment of other plants. Some are agricultural weeds that make it into our gardens. Some hitched a ride from their native areas and find our gardens to be great homes. Some are native species that are kept in balance in their natural habitats, but don't belong in our garden.

Mostly they come up early (think quack grass), spread quickly (quack grass again), have a ton of seeds to blow away in the wind (foxtail and quack grass), and are a ton of work to keep in check because they are rhizomatous (yup, quack grass). I am betting that by now you know the one I hate the most!

So, let's start with my *favourite:* quack grass (*Elytrigia repens*), also called couch grass. This is an introduced perennial, cool-season grass that is now everywhere. It propagates vegetatively as it is rhizomatic, and every piece of root left in the ground is potentially a new plant. It also spreads speedily by seed. In my experience, the only way to get rid of it is through applying elbow grease, and teasing out the roots, being careful not to break them. Then going after it again the moment a new leaf pokes out. You literally have to starve it to death. Have I won the war in my garden? Nope, but I am winning the battles.

Barley, especially wild barley (*Hordeum leporinum*) and foxtail barley (*H. jubatum*), is endemic, and the bane of dog owners. The tiny barbs can get stuck in animals' throats if they munch on them when flowering, and may require veterinary treatment to remove them. The good news is they are fibrous rooted, so they can be dug out readily. They reproduce only by seed, so eliminating the plants before they go to seed is a most effective control.

Bermuda grass (*Cynodon dactylon*) is also known as couch grass, just to confuse us all. This is a mat-forming perennial grass, often found in golf fairways, parks, and, yup, in our lawns. The problem is it also escapes and spreads everywhere via seed.

Smooth crabgrass (*Digitaria ischaemum*) and its cousin hairy crabgrass (*D. sanguinalis*) are frequently confused with quack grass, but they are very different.

Crabgrass is a warm-season, annual species and gets its common name from its crablike growing pattern. It reproduces entirely by seed, so an effective control is to never let it flower, never mind go to seed. If it is growing in the lawn, come spring, make sure there are no bare spots for it to take advantage of. It comes out easily with a tug or levering out of the soil.

Yellow nutsedge (*Cyperus esculentus*) is a creeping perennial with fibrous roots but also long, wiry rhizomes that form tubers at the ends. It spreads aggressively underground, with the potential to increase 3,000-fold in a season.[12] Know it by the yellow umbel-like flowers. Yellow nutsedge is considered to be one of the worst weeds in the world as it significantly reduces crop yields. It prefers waterlogged soils. If you spy it in the garden, get busy digging out the tufts, rhizomes, and tubers.

A number of grasses spread via layering, such as barnyard grass (*Echinochloa crus-galli*), whose spreading, horizontal pattern of growth allows the stems to be in contact with the soil and at the nodes where new plants grow. Other look-alikes are clumping grasses with fibrous roots that propagate via seed, such as tickle grass (*Panicum capillare*), Persian darnel (*Lolium persicum*), proso millet (*Panicum miliaceum*), and even the innocent-sounding annual bluegrass (*Poa annua*).

The trick to controlling grass weeds is to learn their characteristics and methods of reproduction. Then go to work digging them out, making sure they do not self-seed. The goal is to keep them in check, not total eradication, as that is a sure way to the loony bin.[13] —JM

Foxtail barley is a beautiful native grass on the prairies but it has some seriously unwelcome traits.

Grasses for Every Purpose and Location

7

What flowering ground covers may be used as turfgrass substitutes on the prairies?

Let's face it: turfgrass lawns are high-maintenance and require large inputs of water to look lush and full during the hot, dry days of summer. Many homeowners are carefully reconsidering what they use as a ground cover on their properties. Hands down, my top recommendation for a flowering turfgrass substitute is Dutch white clover (*Trifolium repens*). It has a ton of benefits, including:

* It smells amazing.
* It can stand up to low or moderate traffic. (If you need a high-traffic alternative, mix the clover seed with a turfgrass seed such as sheep's fescue.)
* You barely ever have to mow it.
* It doesn't need any fertilizer and barely any supplemental water.
* It will choke out most other weeds.
* It tolerates not-so-great soils.
* It attracts bees in droves.

The big drawback with using Dutch white clover, however, is that although it is a perennial, it doesn't live very long—you usually don't get more than three years out of it before you have to reseed the whole lawn. Although the seed is inexpensive, there is still the issue of labour—but if you consider the fact that you have just put very little inputs into your lawn for the past three years, it's probably more than worth it.

I also really like the creeping thymes (*Thymus* spp.). There are several cultivars to choose from, including *T. praecox* 'Bressingham' and white creeping, woolly *T. serpyllum* 'Elfin' and 'Magic Carpet'. Like Dutch white clover, they have an attractive fragrance and are very appealing to pollinator insects. They will tolerate a light amount of foot traffic without complaint, and they are also useful as fillers between paving and stepping stones, alongside sidewalks, and in boulevard or curbside plantings. Other plants to consider for this type of use include Scotch and Irish moss (*Sagina subulata*), which are not actually mosses at all but resemble them; bugleweed (*Ajuga* spp.); the creeping stonecrops (*Hylotelephium* spp.);

and moss campion (*Silene acaulis*), again, not a moss but a beautiful flowering perennial. Another good selection is the interestingly named pussytoes (*Antennaria dioica*), a native plant that you may have encountered on the prairies or in the foothills of the Rockies. Bear in mind that these are all ground cover plants, which means they are meant to "cover the ground." They will spread accordingly.[1] —SN

Bugleweed is a creeping ground cover that can tolerate light foot traffic.

Are there any turfgrass alternatives that are drought tolerant?

Brown grass in the summer months when it is hot and dry is discouraging. Luckily, there are some alternatives to plain-Jane sod that love the heat and even flourish during periods of drought.

Plus, there are mixes out there that contain a blend of grasses and non-grasses that will grow into a great polyculture of a lawn. If you go this route, make sure you know which species are included in the mix and the percentage of each so you can choose the best mix for your area.

Here is a selection of some of our favourites. All will do the job of making our spaces green when they should be, and with much less water.

*   Creeping red fescue (*Festuca rubra*) has a very deep root system with fine blades of dark green colour. It spreads slowly through rhizomes, creating a dense cover. If not mown, it will grow up to four inches (ten centimetres) tall.
*   Microclover (*Trifolium repens* 'Pipolina') is low growing, rarely flowers, and can be mown just like regular grass. It is not regular clover, just tiny sized. Microclover exhibits "vegetative elasticity," which means that with each mowing, it becomes denser with smaller leaves.
*   Perennial ryegrass (*Lolium perenne*) germinates quickly. It forms clumps, rather than spreading through stolons or rhizomes. A lawn of perennial ryegrass is an easy endeavour and mows beautifully.
*   Sheep's fescue (*Festuca ovina*) grows upwards of twelve inches (thirty centimetres) and forms tufted mounds. A slow grower, it will need mowing only a couple of times a season. It is great sown overtop a regular lawn or by itself as a ground cover.

Here are some other alternatives that look great and do not need mowing. However, with these choices you may not want to run over them barefoot!

✳   Bearberry (*Arctostaphylos uva-ursi*) is a prostrate, multi-
     branched shrub with small, leathery evergreen leaves. Look for
     the small, pink, urn-shaped flowers in the spring that mature to
     bright red berries come fall.

✳   Creeping juniper (*Juniperus horizontalis*) grows from four to
     twelve inches (ten to thirty centimetres) and literally creeps
     across the ground, anchoring itself to the soil wherever a stem
     touches. Durable and native to our area.

✳   Hens and chicks (*Sempervivum tectorum*) grow into dense
     mats that cover the ground neatly. Occasionally the "hen" will
     flower and then die, leaving her many "chicks" to carry on.[2]

     —JM

*Hens and chicks are hardy succulents with a pleasing appearance and
a fairly rapid growth rate.*

Are there any perennial or annual ornamental grasses that can handle dry conditions?

There are several, which is fortunate as we move into a climate scenario where prairie summers feature prolonged heat and drought, and water use is being restricted by many municipalities. (Plus, even if we can irrigate, we hesitate to do so due to the pricey monthly bill!) Increasingly, gardeners need to find plant selections that are considerate of these factors.

I am merely scratching the surface here, but some perennial selections include:

* Blackhawks bluestem (*Andropogon gerardii* 'Blackhawks'): If you want an ornamental grass that will start conversations, this is it! Tall, upright stems hit 5 feet (1.5 metres) in height and feature a dark purple tint in the summer, turning to a near-black colour in autumn.

* Blue fescue (*Festuca glauca*): There are a couple of notable hardy cultivars of this lovely silver-blue grass—look for the cultivars 'Elijah Blue' and 'Skinner's Blue'. I adore the shimmery, fine texture of this one; it dazzles in the breeze.

* Blue grama (*Bouteloua gracilis*): The tan seed heads of this diminutive, tufted grass are supposedly shaped like mosquito larvae; hence, the reason why it is also called mosquito grass. I have to really stretch my imagination to draw that conclusion, but the seed heads are definitely unusual. Blue grama grass readily reseeds.

* Blue oat grass (*Helictotrichon sempervirens*): This is one of my favourite blue-coloured grasses. It mounds naturally in beautiful, tidy balls that look like they were trimmed to shape; moreover, it is nicely behaved and doesn't spread everywhere.

* Feather reed grass (*Calamagrostis* × *acutiflora* 'Karl Foerster'): Yes, this is that tall, striking grass with the bold tan-coloured seed heads you see nearly everywhere, particularly in urban landscapes. The reason why feather reed grass is so ubiquitous is its impressive adaptability to most soil conditions and tolerance for urban pollution, not to mention its resistance to

most pests. It doesn't need much water or care to look pretty. If you're sick of 'Karl Foerster', try another cultivar, 'Overdam', a variegated type with creamy stripes that turn pink in autumn. 'Eldorado' is a variegated cultivar with bold green and cream-coloured foliage.

Annuals include:

* Fountain grass (*Pennisetum alopecuroides* 'Black Beauty'): Fluffy, dark, nearly black flowers and striking dark green foliage—what more could anyone ask for? When planted in containers, 'Black Beauty' makes a bold statement.

* 'Little Bunny' dwarf fountain grass (*Pennisetum alopecuroides* 'Little Bunny'): This is such an aptly named grass: the flower heads are delightfully furry and creamy white in colour. I love this one in containers—it always garners double takes![3]—**SN**

Blue oat grass is an ideal choice for the perennial border, xeriscape designs, and even rock gardens.

What are some excellent perennial grass selections that love the sun?

When we think of grasses, we think of them out there in the sun. There are so many that just adore being in full sun all day long and many that thrive in direct sun for six to eight-plus hours a day. Here are some to consider for that hot and sunny location in your garden that are also hardy for the toughest location on the prairies to boot.

* Big bluestem (*Andropogon gerardii*) is a tall grass with distinctive "turkey foot" seed heads.
* Blue fescue (*Festuca glauca*) with those spiky steel-blue tufts is great for sunny sites, especially out front where you can see it shine. A popular cultivar is 'Elijah Blue', but there are many to choose from. All love dry, almost sandy soils in full sun. Beware, fescue hates wet feet in the winter or being covered in ice.
* Blue grama (*Bouteloua gracilis*) is a medium-tall grass. To my mind, its seed heads resemble toothbrushes out there in the sun.
* Blue lyme grass (*Leymus arenarius*) absolutely thrives in full sun. Caution: only plant it if you can contain it fully or don't care if it spreads, as it will.
* Little bluestem (*Schizachyrium scoparium*) is native to the prairies and is a cousin to the appropriately named big bluestem. It gets its name from blue-green growth in the spring, which turns mahogany in the fall.
* Ribbon grass (*Phalaris arundinacea* 'Picta') or reed canary grass can be described as robust so long as it has adequate moisture. As a variegated grass, it is stellar, so long as you can control it.[4]—JM

The bold variegation of ribbon grass is a stunner in the garden, but this plant comes with a warning due to its aggressive spreading nature.

I have a shady spot in my garden. Are there any perennial ornamental grasses that will do well there?

Shade can be a challenge in the garden, especially when it comes to selecting showy flowering plants for the space. Why not try some gorgeous grasses instead? Foliage that changes colour over the growing season and pretty flower and seed heads—what could be better in a tricky spot?

* Hungarian blue grass (*Sesleria sadleriana*) has showstopping dark purple flowers that appear in the early spring, followed by creamy white seed heads. These clump-forming beauties reach a flower height of sixteen inches (forty centimetres).

* Maiden grass (*Miscanthus sinensis*) is a gorgeous grass with a flower height of 4 feet (1.2 metres) and features striking flower plumes and seed heads. It prefers damp soil and is tolerant of part shade. Other notable and hardy cultivars of maiden grass include the cultivars 'Huron Sunrise', 'Purpurascens' (also called flame grass), 'Morning Light', and 'Graziella'.

* Moor grass (*Molinia caerulea*) has attractive strappy leaves that arch gracefully and provide an elegant appearance in the garden. Moor grass will perform well in partial shade and is happiest in consistently damp soil. Also check out the cultivars 'Moorflamme' and 'Variegata', as well as the tall moor grass *M. caerulea* subsp. *arundinacea* 'Skyracer'.

* Switchgrass (*Panicum virgatum*) has a tall, upright growth habit. Feathery pink flowers make this grass a standout focal point in the landscape. It is adaptable to a wide range of soil types and is tolerant of part shade. There are also several variegated cultivars to choose from, including 'Northwind', 'Hot Rod', 'Heavy Metal', 'Shenandoah Reed', and 'Rotstrahlbusch'.[5]—SN

What are some annual ornamental grasses that are great for containers?

Annual grasses add another dimension to our containers, whether they are on the ground, mounted on walls, or in hanging baskets. When it comes to annual grasses, they can be the centre of attention as the thriller or the fillers, adding whimsy, bulk, or acting as foils for the other plants. Many can be the focal points for the garden.

Check out the wide selection available for those extra elements that grasses can bring to containers: structure, foliage, flowering, seed, and movement, not to mention fabulous colour!

Note that grasses in containers may not grow to the heights they can attain in the ground due to constricted root systems.

* Black mondo grass (*Ophiopogon planiscapus* 'Nigrescens') belongs in the Asparagales order and is native to Japan. It is a diminutive forest species with tufts of almost black, grasslike foliage, growing slowly through rhizomatic roots.
* Bunny tails (*Lagurus ovatus*) is such a cute grass, with its flowering panicles that look just like bunny tails or powder puffs that last and last.
* Cogon grass (*Imperata cylindrica*), also called Japanese blood grass, is known for its stellar upright purplish-red foliage.
* Feather grasses (*Stipa* spp.) have flower and seed heads that look just like feathers blowing in the wind. Look for Peruvian feather grass (*S. ichu*), Mexican feather grass (*S. tenuissima*), or silver feather grass (*S. barbata*) from southern Europe to liven up your containers.
* Fibre optic grass (*Isolepis cernua*) is a sedge, and what a fun one it is to incorporate in a container. It gets its common name from the small flower spikes at the tip of each stem that look for all the world like the tips of fibre optic lamps. They don't change colours though!

* Hakone grass (*Hakonechloa macra*) is a half-hardy grass for the prairies. It is rhizomatic, but a slow spreader, making it ideal for a container. It forms a cascading mound, with slim wiry stems and leaves, reminiscent of bamboo. I love its variegated yellow-gold leaves. Depending on the amount of light it receives, it can be almost white in full sun or lime green in the shade.

* Hard rush (*Juncus inflexus*) or the variant blue rush ('Blue Arrows') is considered hardy to Zone 3 in Canada. It has an upright form with tough blue-green cylindrical stems and almost blue leaves. Growing upwards of three feet (one metre), it can be part of a large combination container or can be planted in a stand-alone container. Regardless, as a rush, it needs good moisture.

* Japanese sweet flag (*Acorus gramineus*) is a species representing the oldest surviving monocots. Not a true grass, it is closely related to the sedges (*Carex*). What it does have is lovely, sweet-smelling, grasslike, gold-green foliage that is only one to two feet (thirty to sixty centimetres) tall. Place this one close to your nose!

* Leatherleaf sedge (*Carex buchananii*) is a popular hair sedge that looks just like hair blowing in the wind. It forms an up to two-foot (sixty-centimetre) upright clump of bronzy cinnamon-coloured leaves and is easily a thriller in any container.

* 'Little Bunny' fountain grass (*Pennisetum alopecuroides* 'Little Bunny') is known for its fluffy seed heads. It grows to two feet (sixty centimetres) or more depending on the cultivar, with green strappy leaves topped with bottlebrush pinkish-white flowers that arch outwards, just like water spraying from a fountain.

* New Zealand flax (*Phormium tenax*), or *harakeke* in Māori, is a plant known for its fibre for textiles, ropes, and sails. It is a beautiful monocot in the Asparagales order with stunning sword-like leaves in reds, greens, yellows, and copper that make it a great choice for a stand-alone container, given that it can grow from one foot (thirty centimetres) to upwards of six feet (two metres) or more.

* New Zealand hair sedge (*Carex testacea*) has olive-green leaves that turn to copper as fall approaches.

* Pampas grass (*Cortaderia selloana* 'Pumila') is a dwarf version of the towering species. It grows only some 20 inches (50 centimetres), then sends lovely creamy-white plumes up to around 4 feet (1.2 metres). A great statement in a pot!

* Papyrus (*Cyperus papyrus* and its shorter version 'Dwarf Form') is another tall grass sized down for containers.

* Purple fountain grass (*Pennisetum setaceum* 'Rubrum'), along with other cultivars such as 'Fireworks', has variegated purple and burgundy leaves.

* Red hook sedge (*Uncinia rubra*) has beautiful red-bronze grassy-like leaves that drape beautifully in a container.

* Weeping brown sedge (*Carex flagellifera*) is native to New Zealand and other islands in Oceania. It is also known as orange hair sedge and forms a low mound of drooping, fine-textured, bronzy-orange or brown leaves. The cultivar 'Toffee Twist' features arching, twisting leaves.[6] —JM

Fibre optic grass is guaranteed to spark interest when you plant it in your mixed containers!

What are some beautiful grasses to put in my pond?

Many of the best "grasses" to put in ponds are not true grasses at all but rather rushes and sedges, which tend to be water lovers and thus are more suitable for damp environments. This list focuses on non-tropical plants, but some may be only marginally hardy to your region. When purchasing grasses and grasslike plants for your pond, consider the spread of the plants. Some are quite aggressive and may not be what you want for a smaller space. As you peruse the catalogues of aquatic plant suppliers, keywords such as "vigorously growing" should pop out at you as something to think about.

RUSHES

* Blue rush (*Juncus glaucus*): Topping out at approximately two feet (sixty centimetres), this attractive rush has beautifully arching blue-green foliage and stems.
* Corkscrew rush (*J. effusus* 'Spiralis'): This curly-stemmed rush is quirky and stylish. It reaches a height of two feet (sixty centimetres).

What would a pond be without beautiful swaying rushes and sedges?

SEDGES

✳ Bowles' golden sedge (*Carex elata* 'Aurea'): I love the airy look of the slim, arching foliage of this plant. The lime-yellow leaves are a bold addition to the landscape.

✳ White rush (*Scirpus albescens*): Yes, it's in the sedge family but has a common moniker of a rush. White rush reaches a height of up to six feet (two metres), with upright green stems featuring white streaks.

✳ Zebra rush (*Scirpus tabernaemontani* 'Zebrinus'): This is another rush/not-rush in the sedge family. The variegation on this plant is very interesting—white-cream stripes run in horizontal bands down the stems.

GRASSES

✳ Miniature cattail (*Typha minima*): This diminutive eighteen-inch-tall (forty-five centimetres) cattail is adorable, especially when it sends up its tiny, furry seed heads.[7] —SN

What are some ornamental grass selections with extremely showy flower and seed heads?

Part of the appeal of grasses is the lovely flower and seed heads that shimmer in the air and sway in the breezes. All are a pleasure to experience, but some really come through with showy appearances that are just stunning. Here are some to delight you.

* Maiden grass (*Miscanthus sinensis*) has long silvery flower heads. When they go to seed, they are a fluffy silvery grey.
* Northern sea oats (*Chasmanthium latifolium*) are loved for their seed heads that droop from the stems like miniature wind chimes.
* Pampas grass (*Cortaderia selloana* 'Pumila') is a dwarf version that has spectacular feathery plumes that stand erect above foliage in shades of pinkish white through cream.
* Pearl or purple millet (*Pennisetum glaucum)* features stiff purple-bronze flower and seed heads that look similar to cattails, but with a coarser texture.
* Pink muhly grass (*Muhlenbergia capillaris*) has shimmering pink flowers from late summer through fall.
* Prairie cordgrass (*Spartina pectinata*) has finely textured flower and seed heads that are a reddish-pink colour come late summer.
* Purple fountain grass (*Pennisetum setaceum* 'Rubrum'), like its cousins, has plumes that fountain off the stems, but this one has strikingly purple flowers and seed heads.
* Ravenna grass (*Saccharum ravennae*) has impressive orange-tan stiff plumes that look like feather dusters.[8] —JM

Pink muhly grass has bright cotton candy–coloured flowers.

Are there any native grasses that are good to plant on the prairies?

Native grasses are not merely pretty—they are serious contenders for plant GOATs! They can handle the vagaries of their local climate. They often establish quickly. The gardener isn't troubled with finicky plants that require constant attention—native grasses are about as low-maintenance as anyone could ask for. Their value to wildlife and insects is immense, as they serve as food and habitat, as well as places to reproduce and raise young. The use of native grasses helps boost the biodiversity of your garden—a win-win for everyone! Here are a few that you might want to try.

* Green needle grass (*Nassella viridula*): I'm fond of the seed heads of this native needle grass: it is beautifully twisted (and supposedly resembles threaded needles). The flower height can reach up to 4 feet (1.2 metres) and the foliage has a tidy, clumping habit.

* Northern rough fescue (*Festuca altaica*) is found in Alberta but not in Saskatchewan or Manitoba, while plains rough fescue (*F. hallii*) grows in all three of the prairie provinces. They are important forage crops both historically for the bison that once roamed the prairies and now for cattle. The sharp, stiff leaves grow in short mounds, while large flowers are borne on tall (5 feet or 1.5 metres) stems.

* Prairie junegrass (*Koeleria macrantha*): Gorgeous purple and green flowers are followed by bold seed heads. Prairie junegrass reaches a flower height of approximately two feet (sixty centimetres).

* Rocky Mountain fescue (*Festuca saximontana*): Topping out at about two feet (sixty centimetres), this is a beautiful clumping grass with fine foliage. It is quite drought tolerant.

* Side-oats grama grass (*Bouteloua curtipendula*): Interesting bell-shaped blooms hang from the floral spikes of this unique grass. It is a guaranteed showstopper! The flower height is approximately three feet (one metre).

* Sweetgrass (*Anthoxanthum nitens*): Beautifully fragrant sweetgrass is an important plant for Indigenous peoples on the prairies. It is very difficult to start from seed as viability rates are extremely low. Sweetgrass is an aggressive spreader so consider growing it in containers.
* Tickle grass (*Agrostis scabra*): Blowsy seed heads and narrow stems give this grass a shimmery effect in the wind. Tickle grass is adaptable to a wide range of soil conditions but prefers damp, part-shade sites.[9] —SN

Sweetgrass is best started from plugs instead of seed.

What are some tall, bold ornamental grasses that make a statement in the garden?

Sometimes we need plants with big architectural interest in the garden, something that will form the backbone of the landscape and make a huge impact. We often think of large perennial flowers doing this job, but there are several grasses that can perform in the role like true champions. Don't be afraid to envision something large scale with the following selections.

* Fountain grass (*Pennisetum alopecuroides*): As befits its common name, fountain grass has graceful arching foliage that cascades from the centre. The red-brown blooms are long-lasting, and the foliage becomes a beautiful bronze colour in fall. The plant grows to 5 feet (1.5 metres) with the flowers.
* Gracillimus maiden grass (*Miscanthus sinensis* 'Gracillimus'): Hardy to Zone 4a, this maiden grass cultivar has a flower height of six feet (two metres). The striking blooms are silver pink in colour. The foliage and seed heads turn an attractive pale tan colour in autumn.
* Porcupine grass (*Miscanthus sinensis* 'Strictus'): The pink flowers of porcupine grass appear in late summer and are highly attractive above variegated blue-green leaves. Silver seed heads follow the blooms. Including the flowers, the plant reaches a height of 5 feet (1.5 metres).
* 'Rain Dance' big bluestem grass (*Andropogon gerardii* 'Rain Dance'): The foliage of this beautiful, tall, arching grass turns dark red in the autumn and the flowers are a stunning purple-burgundy colour. The flower height of this plant is six feet (two metres).
* Yellow prairie grass (*Sorghastrum nutans*): This native prairie warm-season grass has massive, fluffy, golden seed heads. The entire plant can grow up to six feet (two metres) tall.[10] —SN

Which ornamental grasses have beautiful autumn colours?

As a whole, grasses have lovely fall colours that last and last. Many fade to a beautiful tan colour, and those that remain standing in the winter contribute a beautiful golden hue to our landscape, poking out of the snow cover. But there are many that simply have outstanding fall colours ranging from reds to oranges to burgundies to bronzes that make them standouts. Here are some annual and some perennial grasses to consider.

* Flame grass (*Miscanthus sinensis* 'Purpurascens') has, you guessed it, flaming red-orange leaves in the fall that fade to silvery white in the winter.
* Maiden grass (*Miscanthus sinensis*) develops red stems and leaves in the fall, fading to silvery beige in the winter.
* New Zealand flax (*Phormium tenax*), left standing through the frosts and snows, will provide a terrific punch of purple bronze throughout the winter months.
* Pheasant's tail grass (*Anemanthele lessoniana*) is an annual that initially has green foliage but soon develops yellows, oranges, reds, and even purples mixed into the green that shimmer in the fall months.
* Prairie dropseed (*Sporobolus heterolepis*) has finely textured, arching leaves, forming golden-orange mounds in the fall that turn bronze during the winter months.[11] —JM

Switchgrass is another recommendation to grow for spectacular autumn colour.

This gorgeous prairie garden showcases the myriad of ways grasses can be used in the landscape. (Photo courtesy of Marina Matthes)

Acknowledgements

From Janet and Sheryl:

Our publishing team at TouchWood Editions is such an absolute dream to work with! We are so fortunate and grateful! Massive thanks to Tori Elliott (publisher), Kate Kennedy (editorial coordinator), Curtis Samuel (publicist and social media coordinator), Paula Marchese (copy editor), Sara Loos and Sydney Barnes (type-setters), Meg Yamamoto (proofreader), and Pat Touchie (owner). We extend huge compliments and gratitude to Tree Abraham (series designer).

Thank you to Rob Normandeau and Marina Matthes for providing images for the book.

From Janet:

I just want to say thank you. To all the gardeners who have given Sheryl and me such great feedback these past few years. To TouchWood Editions for believing in us. To Sheryl for being a great friend and partner as we travel this journey. To my family who as always supports everything I do. Thank you all—from the bottom of my heart!

From Sheryl:

There is a lot of turmoil and chaos in the world right now, and many people are struggling in different ways. Some things remain constant and always reassuring, however: the feel of warm soil beneath our fingertips, the scent and sound of a gentle rain, the song of birds in the garden, a good meal made of plants we've grown ourselves. And—of course—love and the appreciation of the generosity and kindness of the people around us. I'm truly thankful.

Notes

Introduction

1. Britannica (website), "Grass."

2. Wikipedia (website), "Monocotyledon."

3. University of California at Berkeley, Museum of Paleontology, "Monocots versus Dicots: The Two Classes of Flowering Plants"; Iannotti, "What Are Cotyledons, Monocots, and Dicots?," The Spruce (website).

Chapter One

1. Alberta Parks (PDF), "Alberta's Grasslands in Context."

2. Rutledge et al., "Prairie," *National Geographic* Education (website).

3. Nature Conservancy Canada (website), "Grasslands 101"; Rainer and West, *Planting in a Post-Wild World*, 71–73.

4. The Land Institute, "Perennial Grain Crops: New Hardware for Agriculture."

5. Hodgson, "Ornamental Grasses That Stay Put," Laidback Gardener (website); University of Illinois Extension, Urbana-Champaign, College of Agricultural, Consumer, and Environmental Sciences, "Understanding Ornamental Grasses."

6. Oregon State University, Forage Information System, "Cool-Season or Warm-Season Grasses"; Greengate Garden Centres (website), "Ornamental Grasses"; In Our Nature (website), "Native Grasses for Ontario Gardens."

7. In Our Nature (website), "Native Sedges for Your Garden"; Alberta Invasive Species Council (website), "Nutsedge, Yellow."

8. Hoffman Nursery (website), "Dig Deeper: Juncus"; Spruce It Up Garden Centre (website), "Soft Rush."

9. Hartzler, "Equisetum: Biology and Management," Iowa State University Extension and Outreach, Integrated Crop Management.

10. Vogt, "Do Native Grasses Help Pollinators?," Dyck Arboretum of the Plains (website); Trimboli, "Plant Native Grasses," Backyard Ecology (website); Johnson, "Doing Less in the Garden Will Help Pollinators over Winter," *Chicago Tribune* (website).

11. Rodriguez, "How Would Planting Grass on a Hill Reduce the Rate of Erosion?," Week&, Hearst Newspapers (website).

12. Tantiado and Saylo, "Allelopathic Potential of Selected Grasses (Family Poaceae) on the Germination of Lettuce Seeds (*Latuca sativa*)," ResearchGate (website).

13. Pratley, "Allelopathy in Annual Grasses," Council of Australasian Weed Societies (PDF); Frick and Johnson, "Using Allelopathic and Cover Crops to Suppress Weeds," Organic Agriculture Centre of Canada, Faculty of Agriculture, Dalhousie University; Greer, "Allelopathic Plants: What Are They, the List, and How to (and Not to) Use Them," Morning Chores (website).

14. Adams and Pelz, *Grasses in the Garden*, 40–41.

15. Brine, "Inviting Nature into Your Garden," GardenLarge (website).

16. Spencer, "Wild-ish at Heart: Naturalistic Planting Design," The New Perennialist (website); Lucas, *Designing with Grasses*, 29–30.

Chapter Two

1. OSC Seeds (website), "Planting Native Grasses and Wildflowers"; Prairie Nursery (website), "Seed Stratification Guide."

2. Grant, Bonnie L., "Ornamental Grass for Sand — What Grass Grows on Sand," Gardening Know How (website); Barnett, "Ornamental Grass Clay Soil — How to Grow Grass in Clay," Gardening Know How (website).

3. Odle, "Fertilizing Ornamental Grasses," Plant Addicts (website).

4. Grant, Bonnie L., "Lowering pH of Grass — How to Make a Lawn More Acidic," Gardening Know How (website); Kokemuller, "What Grasses Grow in High pH and Low Nitrogen?," Week&, Hearst Newspapers (website).

5. University of Illinois Extension, Urbana-Champaign, College of Agricultural, Consumer, and Environmental Sciences, "How to Plant Ornamental Grasses."

6. Grant, Amy, "Ornamental Grass Feeding Needs: Do Ornamental Grasses Need Fertilizing," Gardening Know How (website).

7. Traunfeld, "Cover Crops for Gardens," University of Maryland Extension, Home and Garden Information Center; Beaulieu, "How to Grow and Care for Rye Grass," The Spruce (website).

Chapter Three

1. Wild About Flowers (website), "Sheep Fescue."

2. Lawn Chick (website), "Grass Seed Germination Temperature."

3. Canadian Property Stars (website), "De-thatching and Power Raking"; Kalb, "Should You Aerate Your Lawn?," North Dakota State University, Yard & Garden Report.

4. Sproule, "Fall Lawn Care," Salisbury Greenhouse (website).

5. Sproule, "Early Spring Lawn Care," Salisbury Greenhouse (website).

6. Lutz, "How to Restore a Lawn Full of Weeds," *Architectural Digest* (website).

7. Lord, "Why Doesn't Grass Grow around My Conifer Tree?," The Lawn Man (website).

8. Filipski, "Growing Things Outdoors: Don't Bother with Grass under Evergreens," *Edmonton Journal* (website).

Chapter Four

1. Invasive Plant Atlas of the United States (website), "Common Cattail"; Girvan, "Bulrushes Should Not Be Confused with Cattails," Survival and Bushcraft Techniques, Down Not Out (blog).

2. Moore Water Gardens (website), "Planting and Transplanting Aquatic Plants"; We Know Water Gardens (blog), "Repotting Pond Plants."

3. Spengler, "Feeding Pond Plants—How to Fertilize Submerged Aquatic Plants," Gardening Know How (website).

4. Aquascape (website), "How to Care for Marginal Plants."

5. Grant, Amy, "Winterizing Water Plants—Care of Pond Plants over Winter," Gardening Know How (website).

6. Walliser, "How to Set Up and Care for a Pond in a Pot," Savvy Gardening (website).

7. Pond Informer (website), "The Best Grass to Plant around a Pond."

8. Alberta Invasive Species Council (PDF), "Flowering Rush"; Kaufman, "Flowering Rush (*Butomus umbellatus*)—Invasive Plant Biology and Management Methods," North American Invasive Species Management

Association (website); South East Alberta Watershed Alliance (website), "Invasive Plant Management."

Chapter Five

1. Davis, "15 Edible Grasses That You Can Eat," Smart Garden and Home (website); Mentor, "Foraging Survival Foods," Wilderness Awareness School (website).

2. Heirloom Organics (website), "How to Grow Millet/Guide to Growing Millet"; Government of Manitoba, "Rye—Production and Management"; Grant, Amy, "Homegrown Oat Grains—Learn How to Grow Oats at Home for Food"; Thompson, "Growing Wheat: Bread from the Backyard," Epic Gardening (website).

3. Mumm's Sprouting Seeds (website), "Wheat, Hard Red Winter"; Singer, "How to Grow Wheatgrass Indoors: Soil vs. Soilless," Herbs at Home (website); Ontario SPCA and Humane Society (website), "How to Grow Cat Grass Indoors."

4. Rotkovitz, "What Is a Pseudocereal or Non-Cereal Grain?," The Spruce (website).

5. Climate Atlas Canada (website), "Corn Heat Units"; Government of Alberta, "Commercial Vegetable Production on the Prairies"; National Science Foundation (website), "Wild Grass Became Maize Crop More Than 8,700 Years Ago."

Chapter Six

1. Gardeners Yards (website), "Ornamental Grass Looks Dead—6 Causes (with Cures)"; WhyFarmIt (website), "11 Common Issues That Cause Fountain Grass to Turn Yellow."

2. Dorozio, "Beware Smelly Snow Mould as Your Lawn Thaws," CBC News (website).

3. City of Calgary, "Lawn Pests in Calgary."

4. Planet Natural Research Center (website), "Rust Fungus: Identify Symptoms to Treat and Control Rust Disease"; Song, "Rust Fungus Frustration: Treating Rust Disease," Epic Gardening (website).

5. Lynn, "Homemade Spray to Control Rust on Plants," Week&, Hearst Newspapers (website).

6. Missouri Botanical Garden (website), "Anthracnose of Lawns."

7. Ardoin, "7 Natural Ways to Get Rid of Ants in Your Yard and Home," Lawn Love (website); Grant, Bonnie L., "Ant Hills in Grass: How to Control Ants in Lawns," Gardening Know How (website).

8. Government of Canada, "Chinch Bugs."

9. City of Calgary, "Lawn Pests in Calgary."

10. Edmonton and Area Land Trust (website), "Fun Facts: Gopher or Squirrel?"; Kost, "Everything You Know about So-Called 'Gophers' in Alberta Is Probably Wrong," CBC News (website); Government of Alberta, "Agri-Facts: Managing Richardson's Ground Squirrels"; Smith, "How to Get Rid of Ground Squirrels in Your Yard," Smith's Pest Management (website).

11. City of Calgary, "Voles."

12. Government of Manitoba, "Yellow Nutsedge"; TruGreen (website), "Grassy Weeds"; Connolly, "Quackgrass vs. Crabgrass," The Spruce (website).

13. Bubar et al., *Weeds of the Prairies*, 188–89, 198–99, 212–13, 226–27.

Chapter Seven

1. Antoneshyn, "No Grass, No Problem: Why Some Edmontonians Are Looking for Lawn Alternatives," CTV News Edmonton (website).

2. City of Guelph, "Groundcovers and Lawn Alternatives."

3. Greengate Garden Centres (website), "Ornamental Grasses."

4. Prairie Originals, "Native Prairie Grasses"; Trimboli, "Little Bluestem: A Native Grass for Prairies and Gardens," Backyard Ecology (website); Grant, Amy, "Full Sun Ornamental Grass—Ornamental Grass for Sun Gardens," Gardening Know How (website); Bioadvanced (website), "Ornamental Grasses That Take the Heat."

5. Filipski, "Ornamental Grasses Good Bet for Edmonton Gardens," *Edmonton Journal* (website).

6. Iannotti, "10 Great Ornamental Grasses to Grow in Containers," The Spruce (website); Waddington, "10 Ornamental Grasses That Can Be Grown in Containers," *Horticulture* (website).

7. Hydrosphere Water Gardens (website), "Pond Grasses, Rushes and Reeds."

8. Beck, "21 Ornamental Grasses to Add Unbeatable Texture to Your Garden," *Better Homes and Gardens* (website); Lamp'l, "Growing and Using Ornamental Grasses in the Home Landscape," Joe Gardener (website and PDF).

9. Wild About Flowers (website), "Native Grasses"; Alberta Prairie Conservation Forum (PDF), "Rough Fescue."

10. Sherwood's Forests (website), "Ornamental Grasses."

11. Iannotti, "13 Types of Colorful Ornamental Grass for Fall," The Spruce (website); Jauron, "Are There Ornamental Grasses with Colorful Fall Foliage?," Iowa State University Extension and Outreach, Horticulture and Home Pest News; Clark, "Grasses with Fall Color," Tips Bulletin (website); McKay Nursery Company (website), "Flame Grass."

Sources

Adams, Katharina, and Petra Pelz. *Grasses in the Garden: Design Ideas, Plant Portraits and Care*. Suffolk, UK: Antique Collectors Club Books, 2015.

Alberta Invasive Species Council (PDF). "Flowering Rush." Last updated April 2016. secureservercdn.net/198.71.233.67/yjc.cc8.myftpupload.com/wp-content /uploads/2020/07/FDIP_FS-FloweringRush.pdf?time=1617028665.

Alberta Invasive Species Council (website). "Nutsedge, Yellow." Accessed April 1, 2023. abinvasives.ca/fact-sheet/nutsedge-yellow/.

Alberta Parks (PDF). "Alberta's Grasslands in Context." Accessed April 1, 2023. albertaparks.ca/media/6495682/grasslands-in-context.pdf.

Alberta Prairie Conservation Forum (PDF). "Rough Fescue." Accessed April 1, 2023. albertapcf.org/rsu_docs/rough-fescue-backgrounder.pdf.

Antoneshyn, Alex. "No Grass, No Problem: Why Some Edmontonians Are Looking for Lawn Alternatives." CTV News Edmonton (website). July 13, 2022. edmonton .ctvnews.ca/no-grass-no-problem-why-some-edmontonians-are-looking-for-lawn -alternatives-1.5986312.

Aquascape (website). "How to Care for Marginal Plants." July 27, 2016. aquascapeinc.com/water-gardening/plants/create-a-natural-looking-pond-with -marginal-plants.

Ardoin, Jordan. "7 Natural Ways to Get Rid of Ants in Your Yard and Home." Lawn Love (website). Last updated June 17, 2022. lawnlove.com/blog/pest-control -natural-ways-to-get-rid-of-ants/#9-practices-to-prevent-ants.

Barnett, Tonya. "Ornamental Grass Clay Soil—How to Grow Grass in Clay." Gardening Know How (website). Last updated June 18, 2021. gardeningknowhow .com/ornamental/foliage/ornamental-grass/ornamental-grass-clay-soil.htm.

Beaulieu, David. "How to Grow and Care for Rye Grass." The Spruce (website). Last updated March 10, 2023. thespruce.com/all-about-winter-rye-grass-5196072.

Beck, Andrea. "21 Ornamental Grasses to Add Unbeatable Texture to Your Garden," *Better Homes and Gardens* (website). Last updated January 24, 2023. bhg.com/gardening/flowers/perennials/ornamental-grasses/.

Bioadvanced (website). "Ornamental Grasses That Take the Heat." Accessed April 1, 2023. bioadvanced.com/ornamental-grasses-take-heat.

Brine, Duncan. "Inviting Nature into Your Garden." GardenLarge (website). 2011. gardenlarge.com/duncan-and-julia-brine/duncan-brine/on-naturalistic-design-in -the-american-gardener/.

Britannica (website). "Grass." Last updated March 23, 2023. britannica.com/plant/grass.

Bubar, Carol J., Susan J. McColl, and Linda M. Hall. *Weeds of the Prairies*. Edmonton: Alberta Agriculture, Food, and Rural Development, 2000.

Canadian Property Stars (website). "De-thatching and Power Raking." Accessed April 1, 2023. canadianpropertystars.com/power-raking-dethatching.php.

City of Calgary. "Lawn Pests in Calgary." Accessed April 1, 2023. calgary.ca/parks
/pests/fairy-rings-dew-worms.html.

———. "Voles." Accessed April 1, 2023. calgary.ca/parks/pests/voles.html
#:~:text=Voles%20are%20compact%2C%20heavy%2Dset,by%20girdling%20
roots%20and%20stems.

City of Guelph. "Groundcovers and Lawn Alternatives." Accessed April 1,
2023. guelph.ca/living/house-and-home/lawn-and-garden/groundcovers-lawn
-alternatives/.

Clark, Joan. "Grasses with Fall Color." Tips Bulletin (website). Accessed April 1,
2023. tipsbulletin.com/grasses-with-fall-color/.

Climate Atlas Canada (website). "Corn Heat Units." Accessed April 1, 2023.
climateatlas.ca/map/canada/chu_2060_85#.

Connolly, Kathleen. "Quackgrass vs. Crabgrass." The Spruce (website). June 7,
2022. thespruce.com/quackgrass-crabgrass-easily-confused-lawn-weeds-2153114.

Davis, Denise. "15 Edible Grasses That You Can Eat." Smart Garden and Home
(website). Accessed April 1, 2023. smartgardenhome.com/edible-grasses/.

Dorozio, Jennifer. "Beware Smelly Snow Mould as Your Lawn Thaws." CBC News
(website). Last updated March 12, 2021. cbc.ca/news/canada/calgary/what-is-snow
-mould-1.5944512.

Edmonton and Area Land Trust (website). "Fun Facts: Gopher or Squirrel?"
September 17, 2017. ealt.ca/blog/fun-facts-gopher-or-squirrel.

Filipski, Gerald. "Growing Things Outdoors: Don't Bother with Grass under
Evergreens." Edmonton Journal (website). June 25, 2021. edmontonjournal.com
/life/homes/gardening/growing-things-outdoors-dont-bother-with-grass-under
-evergreens.

———. "Ornamental Grasses Good Bet for Edmonton Gardens." Edmonton
Journal (website). Last updated August 29, 2011. edmontonjournal.com/news
/ornamental-grasses-good-bet-for-edmonton-gardens.

Frick, B., and E. Johnson. "Using Allelopathic and Cover Crops to Suppress Weeds."
Organic Agriculture Centre of Canada, Faculty of Agriculture, Dalhousie University.
2002. dal.ca/faculty/agriculture/oacc/en-home/resources/pest-management/weed
-management/organic-weed-mgmt-resources/weeds-allelopathy.html.

Gardeners Yards (website). "Ornamental Grass Looks Dead—6 Causes (with Cures)."
Accessed April 1, 2023. gardenersyards.com/ornamental-grass-looks-dead/.

Girvan, Alex D. "Bulrushes Should Not Be Confused with Cattails." Survival and
Bushcraft Techniques, Down Not Out (blog). July 22, 2011. cookingforsurvival
–yourdownbutnotout.blogspot.com/2011/07/bulrushes-should-not-be-confused
-with.html.

Government of Alberta. "Agri-Facts: Managing Richardson's Ground Squirrels."
Last updated July 2012. open.alberta.ca/dataset/c5011337-7c7f-4df5-8b93
-3008f4d30fd2/resource/48676e91-2f9a-46f8-bbf3-48f81552ef97/download/6188857
-2012-agri-facts-managing-richardsons-ground-squirrels-revised-684-2-2012-07.pdf.

————. "Commercial Vegetable Production on the Prairies." January 1, 2014. open.alberta.ca/dataset/d34210c4-67df-4332-b266-efd01f0bb10d/resource /e729510d-f8e4-4744-a2ba-e5a7bb1b3064/download/6736200-2014-commercial -vegetable-production-prairies.pdf.

Government of Canada. "Chinch Bugs." Last updated June 4, 2013. canada.ca/en /health-canada/services/pest-control-tips/chinch-bugs.html.

Government of Manitoba. "Rye—Production and Management." Accessed April 1, 2023. gov.mb.ca/agriculture/crops/crop-management/rye.html.

————. "Yellow Nutsedge." Accessed April 1, 2023. gov.mb.ca/agriculture/crops /weeds/yellow-nutsedge.html.

Grant, Amy. "Full Sun Ornamental Grass—Ornamental Grass for Sun Gardens." Gardening Know How (website). June 17, 2021. gardeningknowhow.com /ornamental/foliage/ornamental-grass/full-sun-ornamental-grass.htm.

————. "Homegrown Oat Grains: Learn How to Grow Oats at Home for Food." Gardening Know How (website). Last updated February 8, 2023. gardeningknowhow.com/edible/grains/oats/homegrown-oat-grains.htm.

————. "Ornamental Grass Feeding Needs: Do Ornamental Grasses Need Fertilizing." Gardening Know How (website). Last updated November 11, 2021. gardeningknowhow.com/ornamental/foliage/ornamental-grass/do-ornamental -grasses-need-fertilizing.htm.

————. "Winterizing Water Plants: Care of Pond Plants over Winter," Gardening Know How (website). Last updated April 24, 2022. gardeningknowhow.com /ornamental/water-plants/wgen/winterizing-water-plants.htm.

Grant, Bonnie L. "Ant Hills in Grass: How to Control Ants in Lawns." Gardening Know How (website). Last updated May 22, 2023. gardeningknowhow.com/plant -problems/pests/insects/how-to-control-ants-in-lawns.htm.

————. "Lowering pH of Grass—How to Make a Lawn More Acidic." Gardening Know How (website). Last updated November 8, 2021. gardeningknowhow.com /lawn-care/lgen/lowering-ph-of-grass.htm.

————. "Ornamental Grass for Sand—What Grass Grows on Sand." Gardening Know How (website). Last updated June 23, 2021. gardeningknowhow.com /ornamental/foliage/ornamental-grass/ornamental-grass-for-sand.htm.

Greengate Garden Centres (website). "Ornamental Grasses." Accessed April 1, 2023. greengate.ca/ornamental-grasses.html.

Greer, Tasha. "Allelopathic Plants: What Are They, the List, and How to (and Not to) Use Them." Morning Chores (website). Accessed April 1, 2023. morningchores .com/allelopathic-plants/.

Hartzler, Bob. "Equisetum: Biology and Management." Iowa State University Extension and Outreach, Integrated Crop Management. Accessed April 1, 2023. crops.extension.iastate.edu/encyclopedia/equisetum-biology-and-management.

Heirloom Organics (website). "How to Grow Millet/Guide to Growing Millet." Accessed April 1, 2023. heirloom-organics.com/guide/va/guidetogrowingmillet.html.

140

Hodgson, Larry. "Ornamental Grasses That Stay Put." Laidback Gardener (website). June 23, 2015. laidbackgardener.blog/2015/06/23/ornamental-grasses -that-stay-put/.

Hoffman Nursery (website). "Dig Deeper: Juncus." Accessed April 1, 2023. hoffmannursery.com/juncus.

Hydrosphere Water Gardens (website). "Pond Grasses, Rushes and Reeds." Accessed April 1, 2023. pondexperts.ca/Pond-Grasses-Rushes-&-Reeds-c4557005.

Iannotti, Marie. "10 Great Ornamental Grasses to Grow in Containers." The Spruce (website). Last updated December 2, 2021. thespruce.com/ornamental -grasses-for-containers-4141562.

———."13 Types of Colorful Ornamental Grass for Fall." The Spruce (website). December 2, 2020. thespruce.com/fall-ornamental-grasses-4147648.

———."What Are Cotyledons, Monocots, and Dicots?" The Spruce (website). December 14, 2022. thespruce.com/what-are-cotyledons-monocots-and -dicots-1403098.

In Our Nature (website). "Native Grasses for Ontario Gardens." Accessed April 1, 2023. inournature.ca/native-grasses-for-ontario-gardens.

———. "Native Sedges for Your Garden." Accessed April 1, 2023. inournature.ca /native-sedges-for-your-garden.

Invasive Plant Atlas of the United States (website). "Common Cattail." Accessed April 1, 2023. invasiveplantatlas.org/subject.html?sub=6565.

Jauron, Richard. "Are There Ornamental Grasses with Colorful Fall Foliage?" Iowa State University Extension and Outreach, Horticulture and Home Pest News. Accessed April 1, 2023. hortnews.extension.iastate.edu/faq/are-there-ornamental -grasses-colorful-fall-foliage.

Johnson, Tim. "Doing Less in the Garden Will Help Pollinators over Winter." *Chicago Tribune* (website). November 21, 2019. chicagotribune.com/lifestyles/home-and -garden/ct-home-1128-garden-qa-20191122 -ksef7vknmjc6zp55bntkhoy5ye-story.html.

Kalb, Tom. "Should You Aerate Your Lawn?" North Dakota State University, Yard & Garden Report. August 18, 2017. ag.ndsu.edu/yardandgardenreport/2017-08-18 /should-you-aerate-your-lawn.

Kaufman, Sylvan. "Flowering Rush (*Butomus umbellatus*)—Invasive Plant Biology and Management Methods." North American Invasive Species Management Association (website). December 1, 2021. naisma.org/2021/12/01/flowering-rush -butomus-umbellatus-invasive-plant-biology -management/.

Kokemuller, Jill. "What Grasses Grow in High pH and Low Nitrogen?" Week&, Hearst Newspapers (website). Updated January 13, 2013. homeguides.sfgate.com /grasses-grow-high-ph-low-nitrogen-60729.html.

Kost, Hannah. "Everything You Know about So-Called 'Gophers' in Alberta Is Probably Wrong." cbc News (website). Last updated October 30, 2020. cbc.ca /news/canada/calgary/gophers-richardson-ground-squirrel-gail-michener-lethbridge -zoology-1.5782301.

Lamp'l, Joe. "Growing and Using Ornamental Grasses in the Home Landscape." Joe Gardener (website and PDF). 2020. joegardener.com/wp-content /uploads/2020/10/Ornamental-Grasses-Guide-reduced.pdf.

Land Institute, The. "Perennial Grain Crops: New Hardware for Agriculture." Accessed April 1, 2023. landinstitute.org/our-work/perennial-crops/.

Lawn Chick (website). "Grass Seed Germination Temperature." September 18, 2019. lawnchick.com/grass-seed-germination-temperature/.

Lord, Kris. "Why Doesn't Grass Grow around My Conifer Tree?" The Lawn Man (website). August 22, 2014. thelawnman.co.uk/growing-lawn-around-a-conifer-tree/.

Lucas, Neil. *Designing with Grasses*. Portland, OR: Timber Press, 2011.

Lutz, Amanda. "How to Restore a Lawn Full of Weeds." *Architectural Digest* (website). May 13, 2023. architecturaldigest.com/reviews/lawn/my-lawn-is-all-weeds.

Lynn, Audrey. "Homemade Spray to Control Rust on Plants." Week&, Hearst Newspapers (website). Last updated December 15, 2018. homeguides.sfgate.com /homemade-spray-control-rust-plants-32703.html.

McKay Nursery Company. "Flame Grass." Accessed April 1, 2023. mckaynursery .com/flame-grass#:~:text=Flame%20Grass%20(Miscanthus%20purpurascens)%20 is,persist%20throughout%20the%20winter%20months.

Mentor, Coyote. "Foraging Survival Foods." Wilderness Awareness School (website). March 25, 2020. wildernessawareness.org/articles/survival-food-plants -cattail-acorns-grasses-and-conifers/.

Missouri Botanical Garden (website). "Anthracnose of Lawns." Accessed April 1, 2023. missouribotanicalgarden.org/gardens-gardening/your-garden/help-for-the -home-gardener/advice-tips-resources/pests-and-problems/diseases/anthracnose /anthracnose-of-lawns#:~:text=Anthracnose%20is%20usually%20associated%20 with,of%20bentgrass%20and%20annual%20bluegrass.

Moore Water Gardens (website). "Planting and Transplanting Aquatic Plants." Accessed April 1, 2023. moorewatergardens.com/water-gardening-101/planting -transplanting-aquatic-plants/.

Mumm's Sprouting Seeds (website). "Wheat, Hard Red Winter." Accessed April 1, 2023. sprouting.com/product/wheat-hard-red-winter/.

National Science Foundation (website). "Wild Grass Became Maize Crop More Than 8,700 Years Ago." March 23, 2009. nsf.gov/news/news_summ.jsp?cntn_id=114445.

Nature Conservancy Canada (website). "Grasslands 101." Accessed April 1, 2023. natureconservancy.ca/en/what-we-do/resource-centre/conservation-101/grasslands .html.

Odle, Teresa. "Fertilizing Ornamental Grasses." Plant Addicts (website). November 14, 2020. plantaddicts.com/fertilizing-ornamental-grasses/.

Ontario SPCA and Humane Society (website). "How to Grow Cat Grass Indoors." May 26, 2020. ontariospca.ca/blog/how-to-grow-cat-grass-indoors/.

Oregon State University, Forage Information System. "Cool-Season or Warm-Season Grasses." Accessed April 1, 2023. forages.oregonstate.edu/regrowth/how-does-grass-grow/grass-types/cool-season-or-warm-season-grasses.

OSC Seeds (website). "Planting Native Grasses and Wildflowers." Accessed April 1, 2023. oscseeds.com/resources/how-to-grow-guides/planting-native-grasses-wildflowers/.

Planet Natural Research Center (website). "Rust Fungus: Identify Symptoms to Treat and Control Rust Disease." Accessed April 1, 2023. planetnatural.com/pest-problem-solver/plant-disease/common-rust/.

Pond Informer (website). "The Best Grass to Plant around a Pond." Last updated 2023. pondinformer.com/grasses-to-plant-around-ponds/.

Prairie Nursery (website). "Seed Stratification Guide." Accessed April 1, 2023. prairienursery.com/resources-guides/seed-stratification/.

Prairie Originals (website). "Native Prairie Grasses." Accessed April 1, 2023. prairieoriginals.com/grasses.php.

Pratley, J.E. "Allelopathy in Annual Grasses." Council of Australasian Weed Societies (PDF). 1996. caws.org.nz/PPQ1112/PPQ%2011-S1%20pp213-214%20Pratley.pdf.

Rainer, Thomas, and Claudia West. *Planting in a Post-Wild World: Designing Plant Communities for Resilient Landscapes.* Portland, OR: Timber Press, 2015.

Rodriguez, Amy. "How Would Planting Grass on a Hill Reduce the Rate of Erosion?" Week&, Hearst Newspapers (website). Updated August 27, 2012. weekand.com/home-garden/article/would-planting-grass-hill-change-rate-erosion-18069436.php.

Rotkovitz, Miri. "What Is a Pseudocereal or Non-Cereal Grain?" The Spruce Eats (website). Last updated January 19, 2023. thespruceeats.com/what-is-a-pseudocereal-1664721.

Rutledge, Kim, Melissa McDaniel, Santani Teng, Hilary Hall, Tara Ramroop, Erin Sprout, Jeff Hunt, Diane Boudreau, and Hilary Costa. "Prairie." *National Geographic* Education (website). Last updated May 4, 2023. education.nationalgeographic.org/resource/prairie/.

Sherwood's Forests (website). "Ornamental Grasses." Accessed April 1, 2023. sherwoods-forests.com/Trees/Grasses/Grasses.html.

Singer, Francesca. "How to Grow Wheatgrass Indoors: Soil vs. Soilless." Herbs at Home (website). Accessed April 1, 2023. herbsathome.co/how-to-grow-wheatgrass-indoors/.

Smith, Zach. "How to Get Rid of Ground Squirrels in Your Yard." Smith's Pest Management (website). Updated May 10, 2023. smithspestmanagement.com/blog/post/how-to-get-rid-of-ground-squirrels/.

Song, Huan. "Rust Fungus Frustration: Treating Rust Disease." Epic Gardening (website). February 22, 2021. epicgardening.com/rust-fungus/.

South East Alberta Watershed Alliance (website). "Invasive Plant Management." Accessed April 1, 2023. seawa.ca/take-action/invasive-plant-management.

Spencer, Tony. "Wild-ish at Heart: Naturalistic Planting Design." The New Perennialist (website). June 22, 2017. thenewperennialist.com/wild-ish-at-heart-naturalistic-planting-design/.

Spengler, Teo. "Feeding Pond Plants—How to Fertilize Submerged Aquatic Plants." Gardening Know How (website). Last updated November 13, 2021. gardeningknowhow.com/ornamental/water-plants/wgen/feeding-pond-plants.htm.

Sproule, Rob. "Early Spring Lawn Care." Salisbury Greenhouse (website). Accessed April 1, 2023. salisburygreenhouse.com/early-spring-lawn-care/.

———. "Fall Lawn Care." Salisbury Greenhouse (website). Accessed April 1, 2023. salisburygreenhouse.com/fall-lawn-care/.

Spruce It Up Garden Centre (website). "Soft Rush." Accessed April 1, 2023. plants.spruceitupgardencentre.com/11050013/Plant/7378/Soft_Rush/.

Tantiado, Rey G., and Monalie Saylo. "Allelopathic Potential of Selected Grasses (Family Poaceae) on the Germination of Lettuce Seeds (*Latuca sativa*)." ResearchGate (website). January 2012. researchgate.net/publication/267378905_Allelopathic_Potential_of_Selected_Grasses_Family_Poaceae_on_the_Germination_of_Lettuce_Seeds_Lactuca_sativa.

Thompson, Alicia. "Growing Wheat: Bread from the Backyard." Epic Gardening (website). Last updated October 8, 2021. epicgardening.com/growing-wheat/#:~:text=Wheat%20grows%20best%20in%20full,square%20foot%20can%20be%20done.

Traunfeld, Jon. "Cover Crops for Gardens." University of Maryland Extension, Home and Garden Information Center. Last updated February 17, 2023. extension.umd.edu/resource/cover-crops-gardens.

Trimboli, Shannon. "Little Bluestem: A Native Grass for Prairies and Gardens." Backyard Ecology (website). January 19, 2021. backyardecology.net/little-bluestem-a-native-grass-for-prairies-and-gardens/.

———. "Plant Native Grasses." Backyard Ecology (website). July 30, 2019. backyardecology.net/plant-native-grasses/.

TruGreen (website). "Grassy Weeds." Accessed April 1, 2023. trugreen.com/lawn-care-101/learning-center/grassy-weeds?new18=1&var301=v2.

University of California at Berkeley, Museum of Paleontology. "Monocots versus Dicots: The Two Classes of Flowering Plants." Accessed April 1, 2023. ucmp.berkeley.edu/glossary/gloss8/monocotdicot.html.

University of Illinois Extension, Urbana-Champaign, College of Agricultural, Consumer, and Environmental Sciences. "How to Plant Ornamental Grasses." Accessed April 1, 2023. web.extension.illinois.edu/grasses/howtoplant.cfm.

———. "Understanding Ornamental Grasses." Accessed April 1, 2023. web.extension.illinois.edu/grasses/understanding.cfm.

Vogt, Scott. "Do Native Grasses Help Pollinators?" Dyck Arboretum of the Plains (website). July 18, 2017. dyckarboretum.org/native-grasses-help-pollinators/.

Waddington, Elizabeth. "10 Ornamental Grasses That Can Be Grown in Containers." *Horticulture* (website). Last updated March 30, 2023. horticulture.co.uk/ornamental-grasses-for-containers/.

Walliser, Jessica. "How to Set Up and Care for a Pond in a Pot." Savvy Gardening (website). Accessed April 1, 2023. savvygardening.com/container-water-garden/.

We Know Water Gardens (blog) . "Repotting Pond Plants." October 29, 2019. weknowwatergardens.com.au/blogs/news/repotting-pond-plants.

WhyFarmIt (website). "11 Common Issues That Cause Fountain Grass to Turn Yellow." Accessed April 1, 2023. whyfarmit.com/fountain-grass-turning-yellow/.

Wikipedia (website). "Monocotyledon." Accessed April 1, 2023. en.wikipedia.org/wiki/Monocotyledon.

Wild About Flowers (website). "Native Grasses." Accessed April 1, 2023. wildaboutflowers.ca/native_grasses.php.

———. "Sheep Fescue." Accessed April 1, 2023. wildaboutflowers.ca/plant_detail.php?Sheep-Fescue-153.

Index

Page numbers in italics refer to photographs.

© Steve Melrose

About the Authors

SHERYL NORMANDEAU was born and raised in the Peace Country region of northern Alberta and has made Calgary her home since 1994. A writer and master gardener, Sheryl holds a bachelor's degree in English, as well as a Prairie Horticulture Certificate and an Urban Sustainable Agriculture Certificate. Since 2013, she has served as the online Ask an Expert for the Calgary Horticultural Society. She works at the Calgary Public Library—besides gardening, books of all kinds are her grand passion! She is a small-space gardener (on a tiny balcony and in a plot in a nearby community garden) and she is most enthusiastic about growing veggies. She lives with her husband, Rob, and their rescue cat Smudge. Find Sheryl at Flowery Prose (floweryprose.com) and on Facebook (@FloweryProse), X (@Flowery_Prose), and Instagram (flowery_prose).

JANET MELROSE was born in Trinidad, West Indies, and immigrated to Canada in 1964. She has lived in Calgary since 1969. She is a master gardener and the creator and owner of the successful horticulture business Calgary's Cottage Gardener, which specializes in garden education and consultation, horticultural therapy, and advocating for sustainable local food systems. She holds bachelor's degrees in sociology and history, a Prairie Horticulture Certificate, and a Horticultural Therapy Certificate. Janet is a lifelong gardener, coming from a heritage of English gardening. She has a large garden at home in the suburbs of Calgary that can only be described as a typical cottage garden. She cares for many other gardens throughout Calgary through her work as a horticultural therapist, as well as a bed at the Inglewood Community Garden. She is married to Steve and has two children, Jennifer and David. Three cats, Patrick, Theo, and Mia, currently own their home and patrol against the deer, hares, squirrels, skunk, mice, insects, and assorted birds that believe the garden is theirs, too! Connect with Janet on Facebook (@Calgarys-Cottage-Gardener), X (@CalCottageGrdnr), and Instagram (CalgarysCottageGardener).

About the Series

You've discovered the Guides for the Prairie Gardener! This budding series puts the combined knowledge of two lifelong prairie gardeners at your grubby fingertips. Whether you've just cleared a few square feet for your first bed of veggies or are a seasoned green thumb stumped by that one cultivar you can't seem to master, we think you'll find Janet and Sheryl the ideal teachers. These slim but mighty volumes, handsomely designed, make great companions at the height of summer in the garden trenches and during cold winter days planning the next season. With regional expertise, elegance, and a sense of humour, Janet and Sheryl take your questions and turn them into prairie gardening inspiration. For more information, visit touchwoodeditions.com/guidesprairiegardener.